REFORmation and revolution UTION

1500-1800

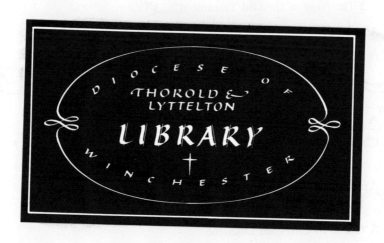

TEF Study Guides

This series is sponsored and subsidized by the Theological Education Fund in response to requests from Africa, Asia, the Caribbean, and the Pacific. The books are prepared by and in consultation with theological teachers in those areas. Special attention is given to problems of interpretation and application arising there as well as in the West, and to the particular needs of students using English as a second language.

General Editor: Daphne Terry

ALREADY PUBLISHED

1. A Guide to the Parables
2. A Guide to St Mark's Gospel
3. A Guide to the Book of Genesis
4. A Guide to the Book of Amos
5. Church History 1: The First Advance
6. A Guide to Psalms
7. Old Testament Introduction 1: History of Israel
8. Church History 2: Setback and Recovery
9. Applied Theology 1: 'Go, . . . and make disciples'
10. Old Testament Introduction 2: The Books of the Old Testament
11. A Guide to Romans
12. A Guide to Religions

IN PREPARATION

Old Testament Introduction
   3 Theology of the Old Testament

A Guide to Exodus

A Guide to Isaiah
   1 Chapters 1–39
   2 Chapters 40–66

A Guide to 1 Corinthians

Church History
   4 The Church Worldwide

Applied Theology
   2 'Feed my sheep'

A Guide to Christian Doctrine

TEF Study Guide 14

CHURCH HISTORY 3
NEW MOVEMENTS
Reform : Rationalism : Revolution
1500–1800

ALAN THOMSON

PUBLISHED IN
ASSOCIATION WITH THE
UNITED SOCIETY FOR CHRISTIAN LITERATURE
FOR THE
THEOLOGICAL EDUCATION FUND

LONDON
S·P·C·K
1976

First published in 1976
by the S.P.C.K.
Holy Trinity Church
Marylebone Road, London, NW1 4DU

Made and printed in Great Britain by
The Camelot Press Ltd, Southampton

The design on the cover of this book is taken from Luther's seal. He described it as: a black cross for mortification, a white rose for faith, a blue field for heavenly joy, and a ring of gold for everlasting blessedness.

The photographs and prints which illustrate this book are reproduced by courtesy of The Mansell Collection, London.

ISBN 0 281 02929 6 (net edition)
ISBN 0 281 02930 X (non-net edition for Africa, Asia, S. Pacific, and Caribbean)

Contents

Preface   ix

Editor's Note: The plan and use of this Book   xi

Bibliography   xiii

Introduction   A Renewed Church in a New Europe   1

Chapter 1   Martin Luther   3
    Martin Luther   4
    Luther's Reformation   7
    The Reformation Divides   11
    Luther's Ideas   12
    The World of the Reformation   13

Chapter 2   Reformation in Switzerland   18
    Ulrich Zwingli   19
    John Calvin   21
    Calvin Defends the Reformed Faith   28

Chapter 3   Radical Reformers   31
    Reformation from below   33
    Trouble at Wittenburg   34
    Thomas Müntzer   35
    Baptism in Zürich   38
    The Faith of the Anabaptists   39
    Catastrophe at Münster   43
    Servetus and the Evangelical Rationalists   43
    The Radical Reformers' continuing Influence   44
    Changing Ways of Worship   45

Chapter 4   Reformation in England   50
    King Henry takes a New Wife   50
    Four Thomases   53
    Protestantism and Reaction   55
    Establishment of the Church of England   58
    The Puritan Movement   60
    The English Prayer Book   62
    Reformation in Scotland   65

Chapter 5 **Catholic Reformation**   67
New Monastic Orders   68
The Jesuits   68
Reforms in Administration   71
The Council of Trent   73
The Decrees of Trent   74
The Roman Church in 1600   75

Chapter 6 **Mission or Empire?**   80
Portugal looks East   80
The *Padroado*   81
Spain looks West   82
Francis Xavier SJ   84
Spanish Missions in America   85
Evangelization of the Philippines   88
French Exploration and Missions   89
Dutch and English Colonization   89

Chapter 7 **American Puritanism**   92
The First Two English Colonies   92
The Massachusetts Bay Colony   95
Two 'Troublers of Israel'   95
New England Puritanism   97
Growth of Denominationalism   98
Some American Denominations   100
The Wall of Separation   102

Chapter 8 **A 'Rational and Practical' Christianity**   105
Christianity and Philosophy   105
Rational Religion   107
Pietist Christianity   109
Pietism and Methodism   112

Chapter 9 **Movements in the Roman Catholic Church**   118
Two Saints   118
Jansenism   121
Gallicanism   122
Suppression of the Jesuits   124
The State of the Church   125

Chapter 10 Asian and Orthodox Christianity 127
    India and Ceylon 127
    The South-east Asian Mainland 129
    The 'East Indies' 130
    The Philippines 131
    China 132
    Korea and Japan 136
    The Near East 137
    The Russian Orthodox Church 138

Conclusion   The Foundations of the Worldwide Church 142

Key to Study Suggestions 149

Index 155

Illustrations, maps, and charts

ILLUSTRATIONS

1.1	Desiderius Erasmus	5
1.2	Martin Luther	8
2.1	Ulrich Zwingli	20
2.2	Geneva in 1551	22
2.3	John Calvin	27
3.1	Thomas Müntzer	37
3.2	Miguel Servetus	37
3.3	Anabaptists at the Lord's Supper	41
4.1	King Henry VIII of England	51
4.2	Sir Thomas More and family	54
4.3	Thomas Cranmer	63
4.4	The burning of Cranmer	63
5.1	Ignatius de Loyola, founder of the Jesuits	69
5.2	St Ignatius in glory	69
5.3	Pope Paul III	72
5.4	The Council of Trent	77
6.1	Francisco Pizarro	83
6.2	Spaniards under Pizarro maltreating Peruvians	83
7.1	Pilgrim Fathers landing at Plymouth	94
8.1	Louis XIV visits the Observatory	106
8.2	John Wesley	113
8.3	George Whitefield preaching at Leeds	113
9.1	St Vincent de Paul	119
10.1	Matteo Ricci and Ly Paulus	134

MAPS

| 1 | Europe after the Peace of Westphalia | 32 |
| 2 | Mission and Empire: Areas of patronage | 87 |

CHART

| 1 | Time line: 1500–1800 | 144–147 |

Preface

Each of the first two volumes in this course describes a complete age in Christian history. The present volume simply sets the stage for the description of the modern Church of the nineteenth and twentieth centuries, which is given separately, in the fourth volume.

I would like to dedicate this book to a former Director of the Theological Education Fund, Erik W. Nielsen, friend, scholar, gadfly, Christian in the grand Danish tradition of Søren Kierkegaard. His zeal for the living faith and commitment to the Churches of Africa and Asia inspired this book and me.

The material on changing ways of worship (pp. 45–47) and the English Prayer Book (pp. 62–65) was provided by Professor Peyton Craighill of Tainan Theological Seminary, Taiwan, to whom I am most grateful.

My tutor in textbook writing for three continents, the editor of this series, played a role amounting almost to co-authorship. The contents and judgements are mine; if it is a usable, readable, and balanced text, much of the credit goes to Miss E. D. Terry of the TEF.

ALAN THOMSON
New Haven, Connecticut, USA, 1975

Editor's Note:
The Plan and Use of this Book

The Editorial Group responsible for the TEF Study Guide series consulted widely and at length before deciding how the Church History Guides should be planned. Eventually they agreed on a three-volume course, all three books of which were to have been written by Dr John Foster. But as noted in Volume 2, to our great sorrow Dr Foster died shortly after that book went to the printer.

By great good fortune we were able to persuade Dr Alan Thomson to take on the assignment at short notice. But as the work progressed, it became clear that he could not hope to deal adequately with the growth of the world-wide Church without making the third volume disproportionately long. It was therefore decided to split the period in two. In this volume Dr Thomson examines the great new movements, and the ideas lying behind them, which changed the face of society, as well as the Church, between AD 1500 and 1800. These of course were the movements which led to the immense missionary expansion of the nineteenth and early twentieth centuries, and to the growth of independent national Churches around the world as we know them today. This expansion, in its turn, will be the subject of the fourth and final volume of Church History in the series, to be prepared with contributions from authors with first-hand experience of the areas concerned.

Because the source material for the period is so much more easily available, no detailed list of sources has been provided. But as before, standard reference books are included in the Bibliography on p. xiii, so that students with access to a library can follow up the passages quoted, and study their context more fully.

MAPS, CHARTS, AND PICTURES

Most standard atlases today contain historical maps which give enough background for the understanding of Church history. The *maps* in this Guide are therefore limited to two. Map 1 (p. 32) shows how the Peace of Westphalia settled the religious divisions in Europe more or less as they are today. Map 2 (p. 87) shows the areas of national 'patronage' during the age of Spanish and Portuguese 'missionary' expansion in the sixteenth and seventeenth centuries.

The *time chart* (pp. 144–147) shows comparative dates of people and events important in the history of the Church during the period covered, and the *pictures* are taken from actual portraits, or from the work of artists, belonging to that time.

STUDY SUGGESTIONS

Suggestions for further study appear at the end of each chapter. They are intended to help readers check their own progress and understand more clearly what they have read, and to provide topics for research and discussion. They are of three main sorts:

1. *Word Studies.* These will help readers to check and deepen their understanding of any technical or other special terms which it has been necessary to use.

2. *Review Questions.* These revision questions will help readers to ensure that they have fully grasped and remembered the ideas discussed and the facts presented. The answers should be written down and then checked with the Key (p. 149).

3. *Questions for Research and Discussion.* These will help readers to understand why things happened as they did; to discover for themselves the links between the life of the Church during the period of upheaval which marked the Reformation and the transition from a medieval to a modern world, and the life of the Churches today; and finally to consider how their own actions may affect the Church of the future.

The Study Suggestions are no more than suggestions. Some teachers may want to substitute questions more directly related to their own situations. Some readers may not want to use them at all.

The *Key* (p. 149) will enable students to check their own work of revision; but please note that in most cases the Key does not provide answers: it simply shows where answers are to be found.

INDEX

The *Index* (p. 155) includes only the more important references to people and places mentioned, and the main subjects dealt with.

Bibliography

Readers may find the following books useful for further study.

GENERAL

The Church of our Fathers Roland Bainton. Scribner, New York
The Reformation Owen Chadwick. Pelican, London
A History of Christian Missions S. Neill. Pelican, London
The Reformation and the Sixteenth Century Roland Bainton, Hodder and Stoughton, London

SPECIAL SUBJECTS

Ch. 1 *Here I stand, A life of Martin Luther* Roland Bainton. Abingdon, Nashville

Ch. 2 *Portrait of Calvin* T. H. L. Parker. Westminster, Philadelphia

Ch. 3 *The Radical Reformation* George H. Williams. Weidenfeld and Nicolson, London

Ch. 4 *The English Reformation* T. M. Parker. OUP, London: New York

Ch. 5 *The Catholic Reformation* H. Daniel-Rops. Dent, London

Ch. 6 *Asia and the Western Dominance* K. S. Panikkar. John Day, New York
— *The Conquest of Mexico* W. H. Prescott. Modern Library, New York

Ch. 7 *A Religious History of the American people* Sydney Ahlstrom. Yale University Press

Ch. 8 *The Church and the Age of Reason* Gerald R. Cragg. Pelican, London

Ch. 9 *The Church in the Seventeenth Century* H. Daniel-Rops. Dent, London
— *The Church in the Eighteenth Century* H. Daniel-Rops. Dent, London

Ch. 10 *A History of the Expansion of Christianity* K. Latourette. Harper, New York: London
— *A History of Christian Missions in China* K. Latourette. Macmillan, New York: London
— *Islands under the Cross* Peter G. Gowing. NCC in the Philippines
— *The Church in Indonesia* Frank L. Cooley. Friendship Press, New York.

INTRODUCTION
A Renewed Church in a New Europe

The thousand years of 'Setback and Recovery' which are described in Volume 2 of this series showed how the 'idea of Christendom' became the principle which unified Western Europe, instead of the Roman Empire. During this period Western Europe, instead of the Eastern end of the Mediterranean Sea, became the centre of Christian activity. The ancient Christian cities, Jerusalem, Antioch, Ephesus, and Alexandria, were now parts of the empire of the Muslim Khalif, who ruled first from Damascus and later from Baghdad. The Church continued under Muslim rule, but from the time of the Council of Chalcedon in 451 it was a divided Church (Vol. 1, pp. 140–143).

Islam eventually also dominated the tribes of Central Asia, and overwhelmed the Church in North Africa (Vol. 2, chapter 2). By the end of the thousand years, in 1453, the last of the Roman Emperors in the East died in the last battle to defend his capital, and the last centre of the ancient Church, Constantinople, passed under Muslim rule. Independent Eastern Christian Churches continued only in Ethiopia, the Malabar Coast of South India, and in Russia. Nestorian monks and Franciscan Friars preached the Gospel and established Churches in China, but neither attempt seems to have had permanent effects. (Vol. 2, pp. 41, 42, 86).

Towards the end of the thousand years, three movements began, which made deep changes in the lives of the people and the life of the Church in Western Europe:

1. *New Learning:* The 'exciting happening' called the New Learning, or the Renaissance (Vol. 2, pp. 176–180), together with the invention of printing, raised the level of education and knowledge, and increased people's concern about the world.

2. *New Lands:* In the fifteenth century, Europeans made sea-visits to Southern Africa and Asia for the first time. At the end of that century and the beginning of the next, European sailors learned of the existence of North and South America and the Islands of the Pacific Ocean (Vol. 2, pp. 180–186). Western European trade with these countries expanded, and became the chief business of many countries which bordered on the Atlantic Ocean. European empires also quickly began. In Europe itself Christian Spanish rulers drove the Muslims (and also the Jews) out of Spain; those who remained were compelled to become Christian. After those events the people of Spain found it easy to see their Christian faith and their Spanish nationality as closely related.

3. *New Life:* After the year 1200, many groups in the Church in the West saw the need to change and renew the life and thought and organization in the Church. In different ways monks and friars, rebellious laymen, theologians, and Church officials had tried to reform the Church (Vol. 2, chapters 10, 11). Some important changes were made, but serious problems remained. At the end of the thousand years, in different places and for different reasons, many people still saw a need for reform in their Church, and continued to ask: 'But this time who will undertake the cleansing?' (Vol. 2, chapter 11).

These three movements determined the new shape which the Church would take in 'the new age, the modern age, *our* age' (Vol. 2, chapter 12). The first of these movements, the New Learning, led people to think about the world, their country's history, and themselves in a new way. This new way of thinking, of course, also affected the way in which they thought about their faith. The second movement, the new contacts between Europe and the five other continents which the world includes, opened the way to making the Church really 'worldwide', but at the same time led to the domination of most of the world by Western Europeans. The third movement, the urgent call for renewal and reform, led to a splitting of the Church in Western Europe. This unfortunate and unexpected result, which separated the Protestant and Roman Catholic Churches, led very much later to a fourth movement, which tried to reunite the broken Church. This later movement came to be called the Ecumenical Movement.

CHAPTER 1
Martin Luther

At the beginning of the sixteenth century, people were discussing a number of different ways to renew the Church. In the lowlands along the river Rhine, groups of mystics, both monks and lay people, sought renewal of the Church through personal holiness. They lived simple and helpful lives, and 'practised the presence of God' by thinking about His mercy and about the sufferings of Christ as they went about their daily work.

Many people felt that the attempt of the Popes to create Christendom, by taking the place of the Roman Emperor as the political head of Europe, had been a mistake. It had led the Popes to use the spiritual power of their office for political ends. Some theologians and Church leaders still hoped that the government of the Church might be changed, so that a General Council should govern the Church, rather than the Pope himself. During the fifteenth and sixteenth centuries, the modern nations of Europe had begun to grow strong, and to unify their peoples. Many people believed that the political ruler of each land, and not the Pope, should be responsible for the Church life of his own nation. The various national languages were becoming more important than the universal language, Latin, and serious literary and scholarly writings were being published in French, German, English, Italian, Spanish, and other languages.

The scholars in the universities who used the methods of the New Learning were studying ancient languages and documents, and applying what they learned to the Bible. Many of them believed that not all of the Church's teaching was really based on the Bible and the teaching of the early Christian thinkers. Perhaps a truer understanding of the life and thought of the Early Church would lead to a renewed Church in their own time.

Many people were thinking about change, and working for it, but they did not all agree about what ought to be done. They needed a leader and a dramatic incident which would unite the various groups into one party of reform. No one party ever emerged to unite them. But many of those who looked for a purer spiritual life, freedom from the political control of the Pope, and a more profound, biblical, and scholarly theology, found what they wanted in the words, actions, and writings of a German monk and professor of biblical studies, Martin Luther of Wittenberg.

MARTIN LUTHER (1483–1546)

The idea of the Protestant Reformation was something which came first to Martin Luther himself, and then to a small group of friends with whom he discussed his ideas. Next it spread to some small states in Northern Germany, and finally to the entire Western Christian Church, including groups who fought against all that Luther taught.

We have learned that several groups of people were interested in cleansing or reforming the Church. The theologians of the universities were shocked at how easily the Church could be divided, with different parts of the Church recognizing two or even three Popes at the same time (Vol. 2, pp. 164–166). Many different groups, like the followers of Wycliffe (Vol. 2, pp. 154–158) and Huss (Vol. 2, pp. 167–169), and the Poor Men of Lyons (Vol. 2, pp. 152, 153), felt that the Church had become too rich and too powerful politically. Most kings and princes disliked it when Church leaders tried to interfere in internal matters of government. And some, like King Philip IV of France, took action to prevent this (Vol. 2, pp. 139, 140).

Many also of the great Christian scholars of the New Learning were worried, because the Church they saw around them was so different from the Church they studied in the New Testament. The greatest of these scholars was the Dutch humanist, Desiderius Erasmus. He made a great contribution to Christian learning in this period, when he printed the New Testament in its original Greek language for the first time. This edition, which appeared in 1516, was used by all the Reformers. But the man who actually started changing the Church was Martin Luther, and he had his own ideas.

Luther was born in Saxony, in 1483, the son of a rich peasant who made money in mining, and who sent his son to the university to become a lawyer and so to help his family. Against his father's wishes, Luther entered a very strict monastery instead of studying for his doctorate in law, and there he became a priest, and finally a professor of theology.

Luther entered what was called the 'religious' life because he was worried about his own relation to God. The more he got to know the Church from the inside, the more he felt that the Church was not really being helpful in relating people to God. He thought that if the faith of the Church was set right, matters of the Christian life and the government of the Church would come right as well. Only a good tree can bring forth good fruit. Thus the Reformation, when it came, was first a reformation in the way Christians pictured God. The changes in Church government, worship, and Christian behaviour came later.

Luther was one of the greatest theologians in the history of the Church, but the subject of his academic work was Scripture rather than

1.1 'The greatest Christian scholar of the New Learning was Desiderius Erasmus' (p. 4).
Dürer's engraving, drawn from life in 1526, shows Erasmus at work on a Greek text.

theology. Some of his most important writings were long commentaries on books of the Bible, including the Psalms, Genesis, Hebrews, Romans, and Galatians. In preparing these commentaries, which were often in the form of lectures or sermons, Luther used the best of the New Learning of his day, including Erasmus's New Testament, the Hebrew dictionary of Johannes Reuchlin, and the commentary on the Psalms of Jacques Lefèvre d'Etaples. Luther was like the humanists: he tried to understand the Bible all over again, using its original languages, Hebrew and Greek. He eventually translated the whole Bible into German. He did this so well that it really seemed as if the Bible writers had written in German, and people still use Luther's translation today. Luther studied the Bible in a very intense and personal way, always asking the question, 'How can I find a merciful God?' In this way he became a real theologian; that is, he was really trying to understand who God is, and what God intends for His creatures.

THE DOCTRINE OF MERIT

Luther's concern about what God thought of him was not unusual in his time. Many people asked the same question that Luther asked, and the Church gave them two answers:

1. The first was that they must follow the way of perfection. Jesus told the Rich Young Man: If you would be perfect, go, sell what you possess and give to the poor, and you will have treasure in heaven; and come, follow me (Matt. 19.21). The Church taught that this perfect life could be lived in the monastery.

2. To those who were unwilling to give up everything and enter a monastery, the Church offered another answer. This was that the Church itself had inherited a rich treasure of holiness created by the devoted lives of the saints who had gone before. This treasure was made available to believers through the ceremonies of the Church, and this was the usual way in which ordinary Christians would experience God's mercy.

Both these ways came from the same idea: that God is merciful to all who come to Him with faith and love; that is, those who are worthy of, or *merit*, his forgiveness. To have faith, means to accept the teachings of Christ and His Church. To love is to live the life He commands, either directly and personally, like the monks, or by sharing in the goodness of the saints which was made available by the Church, particularly through the sacraments of penance and the Lord's Supper.

The Reformation resulted from the fact that Luther tried both of these ways and found that they did not work for him, and indeed gave the wrong idea of the Gospel and the will of God. He tried to live the holy life as a monk, and he administered the sacraments and counselled people as a priest. But he believed that although these two ways seemed to satisfy many people, they did not really help them to know and love God. Luther felt that seeking holiness in the way the monks did made him 'curl up within himself'. It made him think, not of God or his neighbour, but of his own soul. And receiving the merits of the saints through the sacraments made people faithful to the Church, but it did not necessarily lead them to know and be grateful to God Himself.

JUSTIFICATION BY FAITH

These thoughts and experiences led Luther to think again about the familiar words 'faith' and 'love'. From his study of the Bible, and particularly of the Psalms and the Letter to the Romans, Luther concluded three things:

1. That 'faith' in the Bible means first of all God's faithfulness to His people, and then the people's own trust in God.

2. That the faithful God makes His people righteous; that is, he sets them on the right path.

3. That 'love' is the people's expression of their thankfulness to God for 'justifying' them (Rom. 5.1).

LUTHER'S REFORMATION

This was what Luther had to say, but he could not stop there. These new ways of understanding the message of the New Testament led him to reconsider the whole of the Church's understanding of the Bible, and also its sacraments and worship. Many people were concerned about these same problems, and were interested in Luther's answers. But when they raised objections, he told them to go to the Bible and look for themselves. He would not accept the rulings of the Popes or the Early Fathers about what the Bible teaches and how people should behave.

Luther expressed the great questions which the whole Church was asking, and the new printing presses rapidly spread his writings throughout Europe. He was providing material for the political, social, and religious questioning of many people. Luther challenged other theologians to debate in his Ninety-five Theses, which he posted on a church door in Wittenberg on 31 October 1517. But this challenge was not answered until two years later. At a disputation held at Leipzig in 1519 neither he nor his opponents won, but Luther showed, somewhat to his own surprise, that he was no longer willing to take the word even of the theologians of the Church, about the meaning of the Bible. He felt that even condemned heretics like Huss might have been correct. In 1520 Luther was condemned by the Church as a heretic, and in 1521 he was summoned to appear at Worms before a Diet

1.2 'Luther expressed the great questions which the whole Church was asking' (p. 7).
This portrait of Martin Luther was painted by his great friend and neighbour at Wittenburg, Lucas Cranach.

(or Assembly) of the Holy Roman Empire. There he still insisted on the right to make up his own mind as to the meaning of the Bible, and was condemned and made an outlaw.

In 1520, while the Pope, Leo X, was still trying to decide whether to risk the anger of some of the German princes by condemning Luther, Luther himself issued a call to reformation in a series of remarkable pamphlets or tracts. In the first of these, called an *Open Letter to the Christian Nobility of the German Nation,* he attacked the authority of the Church. He wrote that the Church was defending itself against the possibility of reform by barricading itself behind three 'walls'. These 'walls' were the official Church laws which ruled:

1. that the spiritual power of the Church might not be judged by any other power,

2. that only the Pope could decide what the Bible meant, and

3. that no one could call a Council or reform the Church except the Pope.

Here Luther reminded people of the failure of 'rule by Council' (Vol. 2, p. 168) in the previous century. And to overcome this impossible situation he made a very radical proposal. He wrote that:

> all Christians are truly of the 'spiritual estate', and there is among them no difference at all but that of office . . .
> whoever comes out of the water of baptism can boast that he is already consecrated priest, bishop, and Pope, though it is not proper that everyone should exercise the office.

Luther felt, however, that at times like those, many new things *were* 'proper'. So he suggested that the Emperor and the German princes should act like 'emergency bishops' to reform the Church.

In another pamphlet, *The Babylonian Captivity of the Church,* Luther wrote as a theologian to other theologians about the sacraments. He discussed the seven sacraments accepted by the Western Church, and said that there should be one or two or three at the most. He said that the substance of each of the sacraments is nothing but faith, and they must not be 'made captive', or used by the Church for its own purposes.

Luther also wrote about the Lord's Supper, saying that the Church had made up its own mind as to what this sacrament means and what happens. Without reference to the Bible, the Church had ruled that laymen should eat the bread but not drink the cup, that the bread and wine are changed into something else, and that an actual sacrifice is performed. But, Luther said, the Bible does not teach these things. He wrote:

> The mass is nothing else but the divine promise or testament of

Christ, sealed with the sacrament of his body and blood. If that is true, you will understand that it cannot possibly be a work, and that there is nothing to do in it, nor can it be dealt with, in any other way than by faith alone.

Each person, also, must receive the sacrament for himself:

Where there is a divine promise, everyone must stand upon his own feet, everyone's personal faith is demanded, everyone will give an account for himself and will bear his own burden.

Finally, after addressing the rulers and the theologians, Luther turned to ordinary Christians in his book, *A Treatise on Christian Liberty*. Many people agree with Luther in his judgement of this tract: 'Unless I am deceived, it is the whole of Christian living in a brief form.' His whole theme is expressed in two sentences or propositions:

A Christian man is a perfectly free lord of all, subject to none.
A Christian man is a perfectly dutiful servant of all, subject to all.

Towards the end of the book Luther explained these two sentences, which seem to contradict one another:

We conclude therefore that a Christian man lives not in himself, but in Christ and in his neighbour. Otherwise he is not a Christian. He lives in Christ through faith, in his neighbour through love; by faith he is caught up beyond himself into God, by love he sinks beneath himself into his neighbour, yet he always remains in God and His love . . .

The way in which Luther explained himself in these pamphlets shows that he was as much a rebel against the Church as Wycliffe or Huss had been. His friends saw clearly that he would be banned by the Imperial Diet, and they arranged for him to be 'kidnapped' and taken to a remote Saxon castle, the Wartburg, for his safety. It was while he was there that Luther translated the New Testament—and also developed chronic stomach trouble.

Disputes among his followers in Wittenberg led Luther to return in the disguise of a knight, and he soon assumed command of the Church there, preaching daily to restore order. It is not clear whether the Elector Frederick III of Saxony, ruler of the state where Luther worked, really accepted his teaching. But he resented the demands of both Pope and Emperor that his famous and popular preacher should be turned over to them for punishment, and demanded that a general council be held to consider Luther's views. So Luther, like Wycliffe, enjoyed the protection of his ruler, and was able to work in safety and die in peace.

The news of Luther's teaching travelled fast and far. Under its influence the King of Denmark began to reform his Church, and in a few years' time had made Denmark the first 'Lutheran' nation. In 1521 the King of England, Henry VIII, who had some learning in theology, wrote a book attacking Luther's teachings on the sacraments. As a result, the English monarchs have ever since been called 'Defender of the Faith'. Unfortunately, from the point of view of the Pope, all but one of the rulers of England since then have, however, defended a faith different from Henry's.

THE REFORMATION DIVIDES

Although Luther's teaching spread widely, it became clear within a year of his condemnation that the Reformation would have more forms than simply a 'Lutheran' one. In Switzerland and Southern Germany, reformers appeared who adopted many of Luther's principles, but who also differed from him in important ways. The Swiss Reformation will be dealt with in chapter 2.

Even within Luther's immediate circle of friends and followers, there were differences of opinion. Luther's return from the Wartburg to Wittenberg, to take charge of the religious situation there, led to a bitter quarrel between Luther and the 'Heavenly Prophets' of the Radical Reformation (see chapter 3).

Probably the most important split in those early years was that between Luther and Erasmus. Luther made much use of the New Learning of the humanists, and many of them in turn were impressed by his teachings. But after a heated debate between Luther and Erasmus on the freedom of the will of sinful man, the majority of the humanists decided to remain within the Catholic Church, hoping to cleanse it from inside.

Erasmus had written to Luther explaining that although man is a sinner needing God's grace for his salvation, it is necessary for him first to *choose* to repent and believe the Gospel, before God will save him. Luther answered in a long book called *On the Bondage of the Will*. He wrote that though we can argue with our minds for a free will, when we pray we know we are not free. God's tremendous mercy in forgiving us so impressed Luther, that he insisted that only God has free will. Sinful man, he said, is like an animal who may be ridden at will either by God or by the devil. From that time the philosophical humanists like Erasmus were sharply divided from the theological humanists, like Luther's follower Philip Melanchthon (grandnephew of Johannes Reuchlin), and the Swiss Reformers Zwingli and Calvin.

In June 1525, Luther married a former nun, Katherine von Bora, who had been converted by his teaching. Some of Luther's enemies

11

have claimed that he started the Reformation in order to get married. In fact his marriage, like his teaching that men are saved by faith rather than good works, was a consequence and not a cause of the Reformation. (Another Catholic theologian accused Luther of starting the Reformation so that he would not have to confess his sins!) Luther's marriage was, however, a sign that the Churches of the Reformation would adopt a different understanding of the religious life from that which the Western Church had held since the Middle Ages.

Following these events, a number of the North German states and free cities came under Luther's influence. A Diet of the Empire met at Speyer in 1529 in order to sort out the resulting religious confusion, and ordered that Catholics be given full rights to worship in all states of the Empire. Five princes and fourteen free cities signed a *Protestatio*, or protest, against this, and so came to be called 'Protestant'. As a matter of fact most European Protestants prefer to call themselves by the more positive and meaningful term 'Evangelical', that is, followers of the *Evangel*, or Gospel (Greek *Euangelion*). The same practice is followed by Protestants in Latin America, and in other places, such as Indonesia, where the first missionaries came from Europe.

The next year, 1530, another Diet met at Augsburg, and gave the Protestants the right to be heard. Three groups presented statements, the largest being the followers of Luther. The statement read by the Lutherans at Augsburg, which was written hastily by Melanchthon with Luther's approval, became known as the Augsburg Confession (*Augustana* in the Latin in which it was written). This confession remains the official statement of Lutheran belief to this day.

LUTHER'S IDEAS

Let us now return to summarize the basic teachings of Martin Luther. Writing for ordinary believers, he spoke about faith and love. In explaining himself to the theologians, he spoke of the terms Paul made important in the Letter to the Romans: 'justification' and 'grace'.

If God is indeed just, then sinful man is lost. And yet Paul associates God's justice with the Gospel, the good news of God's mercy. According to Romans 1.16, 17 the Gospel reveals God's justice. Also, in two of the Psalms (Pss. 31.1; 71.2) we read, 'Deliver me O Lord in Thy righteousness'. The turning point in Luther's personal struggle came when he reached the conclusion that in the thought of these biblical writers, 'righteousness' is not the characteristic of God, what He is Himself, but rather God is righteous because he makes man right. To 'justify' the sinner means to put him on the right path. As we read in Psalm 40.2, 3:

He drew me up from the desolate pit, out of the miry bog, and set my feet upon a rock, making my steps secure. He put a new song in my mouth, a song of praise to our God.

'Then', Luther wrote, 'I was through.' God does not love us because we are righteous, but because He loves us He *makes* us righteous. After that, our whole Christian life is an expression of thankfulness for the forgiveness of our sins.

Luther's thinking about grace is his most distinctive contribution to Christian theology. Grace is not a *thing* which God gives. It is not a peculiar magical power. It is not the 'medicine of immortality', as Ignatius of Antioch called it in the early days of the Church (see Vol. 1, p. 64). Luther's disciple Melanchthon put it in his handbook of Christian teaching, the *Loci Communes*: 'grace is not medicine, but favour', that is, God's favour.

For Luther, grace is God's attitude towards man. It is the 'light of his countenance' (Num. 6.26). Grace means that God is 'pleased' with us, as the angels sang on Christmas Eve (Luke 2.14). Like Mary, believers are 'favoured' by God (Luke 1.28). Thus God's grace is not a thing that may be given, but a personal attitude that must be sought. The difference is that we must not look to things for our salvation, but to God Himself.

Luther here picks up and emphasizes the whole personal side of Christian devotion which was taught by Bernard of Clairvaux (see Vol. 2, p. 149), Francis of Assisi, and the German mystics of the previous century. Bernard, Francis, the mystics, and Luther were the believers who emphasized most strongly that the centre of the Christian faith is Jesus Christ Himself. For Luther, faith and salvation meant simply 'having a God', and Luther found Him in Jesus Christ our Lord.

Luther's reformation brought three things into the thinking of the Church which can never again be forgotten:

1. That the Bible again and again has a new message when we need it.

2. That the centre of the message of the Bible is the relation between God and His creatures.

3. That this simple relationship is literally revolutionary. It changes everything.

THE WORLD OF THE REFORMATION

In the first half of the sixteenth century the world was bursting with new possiblities—and new problems. The problems of the setback described in Vol. 2 continued, as did the promise of recovery. Catholic Christians had recovered all of Spain and Portugal, down to Gibraltar, from the Muslim Arabs. In their overseas explorations as well, the

Spanish and Portuguese planted the Church in the partly Muslim East Indies (now called Malaysia and Indonesia). The Portuguese seized the important Malayan port of Malacca in 1511, and Portuguese friars said mass in the Molucca Islands further east ten years later. Friars travelling with Magellan (Vol. 2, p. 185) were baptizing new Christians in the Philippines. Franciscans helped to establish a short-lived Christian kingdom in the Congo, where, about 1820, the King Affonzo's son Henrique became the first black African bishop.

At the same time, however, the Muslim rule of the Ottoman Turks (Vol. 2, pp. 171, 172) was rapidly extended over the whole of the Balkan peninsula in Eastern Europe. By 1526 they controlled Serbia (now part of Yugoslavia) and Hungary, and in 1529 they attacked Vienna itself. One of the great victories of Islam during this period had a lasting effect. A Tatar empire, called the Moghul Empire, was established in North India. One of the results of this event was the division of the Indian sub-continent in our own time into Hindu India and Muslim Pakistan and Bangladesh.

The Roman Catholic Church also expanded at the expense of the Eastern Churches, which were not progressive during this period. Through Portuguese exploration, contact was made with the ancient Syrian Orthodox Church of Malabar in South India (see Vol. 1, p. 176). The coming of Jesuit missionaries led to the creation, among some of the Christians there, of a *Uniat* Church. A Uniat Church is one which keeps its own separate customs and Church law, but recognizes the authority of the Pope. More than half of the old Syrian Christians became members of this Church.

Another Uniat Church, created a little later, was the Maronite Church of Lebanon, a Church which, in the seventh century, rejected the final form of the Orthodox definition of the person of Christ. This Church is the majority Christian body in Lebanon, the one Near Eastern nation which remains half-Christian and half-Muslim. The president of Lebanon has in recent times always been a Maronite Christian, and the premier a Muslim.

The voyages sponsored by the Catholic nations, Spain and Portugal, led Pope Alexander VI to mark out 'spheres of influence' for them in the world. From 1494 the Portuguese were authorized to build up the Church to the East, and the Spanish to the West. Thus most of Latin America—except Brazil which sticks out over the line—speaks Spanish. Portuguese influence continues in colonies in Timor, Macao, and Southern Africa. The Spanish and Portuguese rulers were given special rights as patrons over the Churches which they built up and supported. By the middle of the sixteenth century there were Spanish bishops in the West Indies, Mexico, and Peru; and universities in Lima, capital of Peru, and in Mexico City.

This 'explosion' of Europe all over the world came from tensions within Europe itself. Economic and social changes were coming, moving in the direction of the modern way of life. As a result of European influence, these gradually spread to the rest of the world. Towns and cities were arising to take advantage of the opportunities for trade which had been opened up by the Crusades in the Mediterranean (see Vol. 2, chapter 6). Possibilities for trade were greatly increased by the discoveries of the Portuguese and Spanish. Money was becoming more important than land, which had been the basis of the feudal system (see Vol. 2, p. 74). Money was used chiefly in the towns and cities, and was mainly in the hands of the merchants, not the nobility.

In medieval society there had been three 'estates' or 'classes'; the priests, the nobles, and the peasants. But now another estate, the traders of the cities, was becoming increasingly powerful. This meant that the land-owning nobility needed money more than they needed the produce of the land or the services which the peasants provided for them in accordance with long-established feudal customs. The resulting uncertainties and violation of customary practices led to a series of peasant uprisings all over Europe. The most serious of these peasant uprisings occurred in Luther's part of Germany in 1524–6. When we think about the political ideas of men such as Luther, we must remember that a phrase like 'the sovereignty of the people' or 'democracy' would be understood to mean rule by bands of uneducated peasants whom they had seen burning, looting, and killing in their hopeless fury. Speaking of the danger of people in a mass, Luther wrote: 'My dear Lords, Mr Everybody is not to be toyed with. Therefore God would have authorities, so that there might be order in the world'.

Europe was changing from a feudal, farming society to a capitalist one of industry, trade, and cities. All large-scale social change is painful, and these pains are the background of the Reformation. It is interesting that the people who were most active in spreading the most radical ideas of the Reformation were weavers, independent small business men roaming Europe, and that the Reformed and Anabaptist Churches arose in the Free Cities of Europe (see chapters 2 and 3).

Europe was also changing politically. The delegates attending the various Councils of the Church were divided into 'nations' (see the idea of nationhood in Vol. 2, p. 5). This meant something rather different from what we think of today as nations. But the idea of nationality was catching hold in Europe and would spread throughout the world. What had been a mass of small feudal states (more than three hundred in Germany alone) was gradually becoming a group of nations under kings. A common language was the main sign of unity. The first of these nations were Spain and France, and in the sixteenth century European politics were dominated by their efforts to dominate each other and the Pope. The most powerful man during the Reformation period was the Holy Roman Emperor, Charles V, who was in the first place King of Spain, and whose family, the Hapsburgs, ruled Austria and the Netherlands.

The people who were chiefly attracted to the Reformation were the 'New Men' of Europe: scholars, businessmen, despairing peasants, and rulers seeking independence from the Pope. Although Martin Luther was condemned by Church and state as Huss had been a century before (see Vol. 2, pp. 167, 168), the political confusion kept him from sharing Huss's fate. The longing for the cleansing of the Church, also, made people postpone taking any definite position on Luther's teachings, in hopes that a Council would settle everything. In 1521 Luther asked to be heard by a Council, and the Council finally met in 1545, after being delayed a long time for political reasons. But by that time it was too late to reunite the Church in Europe.

STUDY SUGGESTIONS

WORD STUDY

1. How did Luther's followers come to be called 'Protestant'? What other name were they known by? Which do you prefer, and why?
2. What is a *Uniat* Church? Find out the names of other Uniat Churches besides the two mentioned in the chapter.
3. Which of the following terms best describes what Luther meant by 'faith'?
   Agreement belief trust acceptance religion
   Explain your answer.
4. Which of the following terms did Luther think that 'grace' in the New Testament really meant?
   the power of God   a mystery   God's favour   human ability
   a gift from God

REVIEW OF CONTENT

5. Which of the problems faced by the Reformation were the same as those faced by the Church in the Middle Ages?
6. What major new problem did the Reformation itself create?
7. Name some groups of people who were trying to reform the Church before Luther's time?
8. What problem did Luther try to solve by entering a monastery?
9. What answers did the Church of the time offer to Luther's problem?
10. Why did Luther not find the Church's answers helpful?
11. Why were so many people attracted to Luther's teaching?

12. What 'three walls' did the Church erect, to keep itself from being reformed, according to Luther?
13. In what way were the sacraments held in 'Babylonian Captivity'?
14. What did Luther mean when he said that the Christian was 'a perfectly free lord of all'?
15. What were the 'estates' of the Middle Ages, and what new 'estate' appeared at the beginning of the modern period?
16. Why did the Humanists finally turn against Luther?
17. Why are English monarchs called 'defender of the faith'?
18. In what way did both the Church and Islam expand during the sixteenth century?
19. Who divided the non-Christian world between Spain and Portugal? Does the line of division still have meaning today?

DISCUSSION AND RESEARCH

20. Christians who continued their allegiance to the Pope were very upset when Luther 'rent the seamless robe of Christ'. How important is the unity of the Church to you? Why? What would you do if you felt that the Church to which you belong was not teaching the truth, or was not behaving in a loving and helpful way?
21. Luther and Erasmus differed as to whether sinners were still free to repent and believe the Gospel. How would you have decided who was right?
22. Can a Church finally take the wrong path? How would you know whether a group who called themselves a Church really were a Church? Can a Church stop being a Church?

CHAPTER 2

Reformation in Switzerland

The Protestant Reformation of the sixteenth century was Luther's Reformation. Although it had its own history in many lands, the leaders everywhere studied Luther's writings. Most of the Protestant leaders who disagreed with Luther felt that he had not gone far enough, or had not been consistent in his thought.

Luther had two basic ideas, which have been the starting point for Protestants or Evangelicals everywhere. They are:

1. that the beginning of Christian faith and theology is that God has made sinners righteous through what He did in Jesus Christ, and

2. that the only sure and dependable source for Christian faith and life is the Bible.

From the beginning, however, the Reformation was not one 'Church', but a group of related movements all influenced by Luther. Luther was not interested in organization or campaigns. He never thought of himself as a founder or leader, but simply as one who pointed out that everything comes from the Word of God, and 'the Word did it all', as he put it. Luther's own work was all done in north-eastern Germany, but his message soon took root elsewhere, and nowhere more quickly and effectively than in Switzerland.

In the sixteenth century what we now know as Switzerland was a collection of city-states, called 'cantons', and free cities, in the southern part of the Holy Roman Empire. The cantons were organized into a loose confederation, which was always a rather independent part of the Empire. Its chief enemy was Austria, the ancestral land of the Emperor Charles. Each of the cantons was ruled by its own city government. They were never a part of the feudal system. Mountainous Switzerland has never been farming country, and its citizens supported themselves by small manufacturing, and by trade. Northern Switzerland was at the centre of Europe's trade, and traders generally are not too much concerned about the religion or politics of the people they deal with. Free cities like Basle or Strasbourg were always well known for their religious tolerance.

Therefore when Luther's pamphlets were read in Switzerland, they were read by small businessmen and craftsmen of the towns, not by noblemen or peasants. The 'Reformed', as they came to be called in Switzerland and France, were more practical and more concerned with organization than were the Lutherans. Their theologians were not such deep thinkers as Luther, but some of them were better scholars.

Reforming the Church was also a little easier in the southern part of the Holy Roman Empire than it had been in the north. Luther could only achieve reforms by persuading the great feudal lords of Germany, and these lords in their turn had to persuade the Emperor and Pope. But the Reformed had only to convince their own city councils.

ULRICH ZWINGLI (1484–1531)

The Reformation in Switzerland was begun by Ulrich Zwingli, a priest in Zürich. He was trained as a humanist, and was a friend of the greatest of the humanists, Desiderius Erasmus. Although he was influenced by Luther's teaching, Zwingli can perhaps be called a 'radical humanist'. (Throughout this book the word 'radical' will be used in the sense of the Latin word from which it comes, *radix*, meaning 'root'. A 'radical' is a person who is concerned about the roots or foundations of things. 'Radical' change means fundamental change, in which everything is altered.)

Zwingli held many of the same opinions as Luther, but sometimes for different reasons. For instance, both Luther and Zwingli believed in 'predestination', i.e. that it is God alone, not what we do or believe, that saves us. Luther believed this because he was convinced that God's love was greater than our sins. Zwingli, on the other hand, believed in predestination because he thought that God was the source of everything that happens, including our salvation. Thomas Aquinas (see Vol. 2, pp. 116–118) understood predestination in the same way as Zwingli did.

Zwingli was a man of action, who several times served as a chaplain with the Zürich army, and was killed in battle. He was very popular with the people of Zürich because he remained in the city during an outbreak of plague, and cared for the sick.

Zwingli began his career as a Reformer by preaching a series of sermons, going straight through Erasmus's Greek text of the New Testament. The two most important of Zwingli's beliefs were:

1. that the Bible is a complete guide to the Christian life.

2. that the chief teaching of the Bible is God's direct rule over the world and human life.

In accordance with the second of these principles, Zwingli taught that we are saved directly by God's will—here he agreed with Luther. But this means that we are not saved by means of the sacraments—this was different from Luther's ideas.

Zwingli believed that the Bible is indeed a complete guide to life, so that Christians are bound to do what the Bible teaches and nothing else. In accordance with this belief, statues were taken down from the churches, and organs broken up. An entirely new and simple worship

2.1 'The Reformation in Switzerland was begun by Ulrich Zwingli—a man of action' (p. 19)—as we can see from this portrait by an unknown artist.

service, based entirely on the Bible, replaced the mass, and congregational singing was no longer accompanied by instruments.

Zwingli was a radical theologian, but he was a conservative and practical man in other ways. He felt that the city council had the right to decide what the worship of the people should be. The theologian's job was to argue for reformation, but until the council was persuaded, he must obey the existing regulations. Zwingli began to speak against the mass in 1521, but tolerated its celebration until it was outlawed in 1525. Many of his followers could not understand his attitude. They rejected his leadership, just as Karlstadt and Müntzer rejected Luther's conservative view of Church life (pp. 26, 34, 35).

JOHN CALVIN (1509–1564)

The greatest of the Reformed theologians, and the most important of the Swiss theologians, however, was not Zwingli, but a Frenchman, John Calvin. Calvin did not visit Switzerland until after Zwingli's death, and he remained an alien there, almost until his own death.

Calvin, like Zwingli, was a humanist before he became a Reformer and theologian. In fact, he never had any formal theological education, and was never regularly ordained, so far as we know. But Calvin's theology became the basis of the life of the Reformed Churches in Switzerland, France, the Netherlands, Great Britain, and North America. Churches founded by missions from those countries carried Calvin's thought around the world.

Calvin studied languages, literature, and law in several French universities, and the first book he wrote was a study of the Roman Stoic philosopher Seneca. Calvin rarely wrote about himself, and we do not know what led him to follow Luther's teachings. We *do* know that he was acquainted with a prominent group of French humanists, which included Jacques Lefèvre d'Etaples. Some of these humanists became Protestants, including Calvin's cousin, who translated the New Testament into French. There were anti-Catholic incidents in Paris in 1534, and Calvin suffered imprisonment, perhaps as a result. He fled from France and moved to the great literary centre of Basle in Switzerland. There he settled down to write a handbook for Protestant theological students, which he called *Institutes of the Christian Religion*.

Calvin wanted to be an independent theological scholar, but the chief preacher in Geneva, which had recently voted to become Reformed, persuaded him that he was needed to help reorganize that unruly city. We might say that Luther and his followers were 'Evangelical', because they believed that the Christian life consisted in understanding and believing the Gospel of God's loving grace, which would bear fruits by itself in the life of the believer. In the same way,

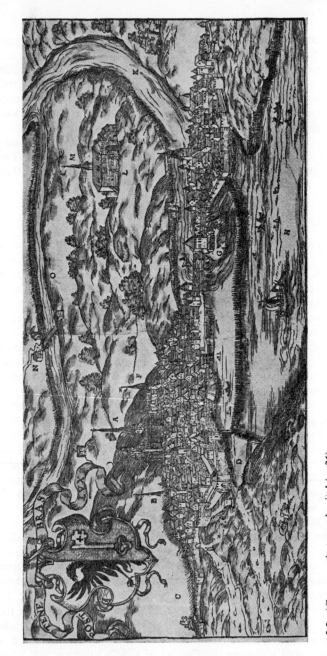

2.2 'Geneva—that unruly city' (p. 21).
A view of Geneva in 1551 shows the important churches there.

the Reformed believed that God's grace demanded definite change or reform in the life of the individual, in the Church, and in society as a whole. Calvin set about this task, amid great difficulties, and helped to make Geneva an example of the Reformed life.

Calvin was invited to become a 'teacher' in the Church of Geneva. The Reformed believed, following Ephesians 4.11, that the 'ordinary' ordained offices of the Church were preachers, teachers, and elders. Calvin organized the Church in Geneva with a board of preachers and elders, wrote a confession of faith and a catechism for children, and opened an academy, which later became the University of Geneva. Students from this academy became Reformed pastors in France, Scotland, England, the Netherlands, and such Eastern European countries as Bohemia, Hungary, and Poland. As a Teacher of the Church, Calvin lectured straight through the Old Testament on weekdays, and the New Testament on Sundays.

Reformers like Luther and Calvin may be considered the first 'biblical theologians', that is, thinkers who attempted to find a system of Christian teaching directly from the Bible itself. They may have been helped in this by their habit of preaching straight through biblical books verse by verse. This may seem a dull method now, but it does help to understand the way of thinking of the biblical writers from the inside. Calvin, like Luther, found Paul's argument in the Letter to the Romans to be the key to the Gospel, the central message of the whole Bible.

CALVIN'S TEACHING

One scholar has commented that Calvin, like Augustine, wrote more books than one man can easily read in a lifetime. But Calvin's main teachings are clearly and fully set out in his big book, *Institutes of the Christian Religion*. This book first appeared as a textbook of six brief chapters in 1536. Calvin continued working on it throughout his life. The *Institutes* went through nine editions in Latin and French, and twenty-five printings. In the end, in 1559, it appeared in four large volumes. These dealt with: (1) God the Creator, (2) Christ the Redeemer, (3) the Holy Spirit and the Christian Life, and (4) the Church. Much of the material added in the later additions was arguments with Roman Catholic and Anabaptist writers (see chapter 3).

In most of what he wrote, Calvin was a good 'Lutheran', basing everything on the Bible, and believing that 'Justification is the hinge on which religion turns'. The movement of thought in the *Institutes* corresponds with Paul's argument in the Letter to the Romans, it deals with:

1. Man's misery apart from God (Rom. 1.18—3.20).
2. God's grace in Jesus Christ which overcomes man's misery (Rom. 3.21—5.20).

3. The new life brought in by the Holy Spirit (Rom. 6—11).

4. The ordering of the new life in the fellowship of the Church (Rom. 12—16).

But the four parts of the *Institutes* also correspond to the parts of the great medieval textbook of theology, Peter Lombard's *Sentences* (see Vol. 2, p. 115).

The really important difference between Luther's thought and Calvin's was that Calvin was more careful and systematic. He attempted to bring together the message of the entire Bible, and of all its many writers, into one logical whole. But Calvin's teaching did differ significantly from Luther's: (a) in Calvin's heavy emphasis upon the Church, and (b) in his view of what happens in the Lord's Supper.

(a) THE CHURCH

New theological teachings usually arise when people are concerned about some aspect of their faith, and feel the need to re-state it. In the Reformation, Christians began to worry about the Church. Formerly people had thought of the Church as one (although the Latin and Greek parts of it had not been speaking to each other for centuries), and as having had a continuous history since the Apostles. But as a result of Luther's teaching, there were now two groups in Western Europe, each claiming to be the true Church. At the time of the Gnostic crisis in the Early Church, Irenaeus of Lyons had said that the true Church was that which possessed the teachings of the Apostles (see Vol. 1, p. 59). But did the word 'apostolic' in the Creed of Nicaea (see Vol. 1, p. 139) in the phrase, 'I believe in the Holy Catholic and Apostolic Church', mean a continuous succession of bishops, ordained successively from the Apostles themselves? Or did it mean faithfulness to the *teaching* of the Apostles as contained in the New Testament? The Roman Catholics took the first view, and the Protestant Reformers the second. Generally, the Reformers said that only three things were necessary for the true Church;

1. the Bible,
2. the sacraments, usually two in number, and
3. an orderly Christian life.

One Roman Catholic theologian, Cardinal Bellarmino, listed fifteen marks of the true Church.

Luther thought that the true Church consists of the real believers, and that only God knows for sure who they are. The Church that we see in the world is a visible institution, with buildings to which people can come to hear God's Word read and preached and celebrated in the sacraments, and so become converted to the true Church, where Christ rules and no rules can be laid down by men.

Calvin, on the other hand, believed the Church to be an institution for Christian education, where people are not only called to repent and believe, but also taught how to live Christian lives in a practical way. For this reason, the ordinary visible Church was very important for Calvin. He believed that it should be carefully organized according to the teaching of the New Testament. He also thought that the Church should have the right to run its own affairs, without interference by the government. The business of the government was to defend the Church, and the business of Christian officials was to obey the Church in their daily lives. Both Luther and Calvin were influenced in their understanding of the Church by John Wycliffe (see Vol. 2, pp. 155–157).

(b) THE LORD'S SUPPER

One thing which all the Reformers and some Catholics agreed about, was that the mass as it was celebrated and understood at the time was something quite different from the New Testament picture of the Lord's Supper. Perhaps the greatest tragedy of the Reformation was that the different Protestant groups did not agree on what should replace it. At ecumenical gatherings today as many as five different services of communion or the Lord's Supper may be held, as many as three of them by groups which arose from the Reformation.

The beginnings of these divisions came early in the Reformation itself. The German Protestant princes, who feared attack from the Catholic princes of the Empire, attempted to form a political league. For this reason they urged their theologians to produce a common statement of faith as the basis for the alliance.

The theologians met at Marburg in 1529. Luther and Melanchthon represented the Lutherans, and Martin Bucer of Strasbourg, a friend of both Luther and Melanchthon, led the Reformed. A statement containing fifteen points was drawn up, and there was agreement on fourteen of them. But on the last, the Lord's Supper, there was no agreement, and the negotiations failed. Luther said to Bucer during the discussions: 'You have a different spirit from us.' European Lutheran and Reformed Churches today are trying to repair this breach.

The official Roman Catholic doctrine of 'transubstantiation', which all the Reformers rejected, was stated by Pope Eugene IV in these words:

The priest, speaking in the person of Christ, makes this sacrament. For by virtue of the very words, the substance of the bread is converted into the body of Christ, and the substance of the wine into his blood.

We should notice three things here: (1) the priest, by what he says, performs the action, (2) the bread and wine are not bread and wine any longer, but their appearance remains the same, and (3) this is a real, objective happening. Laymen were not permitted to drink the conse-crated wine for fear that they might spill Christ on the floor.

Luther agreed that the Lord's Supper is one of the most important acts of the Church, and that in it the real body of Christ is given. But he believed this event occurs because of God's faithfulness to people, not because of the words spoken by an ordained priest. According to Luther, it is God, not the Church, who offers the Lord's body and blood. Nor is the Lord's Supper, as Catholics believed, a new sacrifice of Christ for our sins. It is our communion with Christ. In the Lord's Supper the bread and wine do not change, Luther believed, but Christ comes to whoever eats and drinks, 'under' the bread and wine. So Luther *agreed* with the Roman Catholics that Christ's body is really given, but he *disagreed* with them as to how this occurs.

A number of humanists, among them the Reformer Zwingli, understood the Lord's Supper in another way. They believed that salvation does not come 'by flesh and blood.' They thought that at the Last Supper Jesus acted as the Old Testament prophets had done. As Jeremiah used an ox yoke as a sign of the coming bondage of Judah, so Jesus broke bread as a sign of His coming death. 'This is my body' meant 'this is a sign of my broken body'. Andreas Karlstadt (see p. 35) thought that when Jesus said these words He pointed to Himself. Zwingli taught that the Lord's Supper was a reminder of the death of Christ, a pledge of allegiance to our Saviour, and a public proclamation of the salvation He brings.

John Calvin felt that none of the three explanations given above were true to the account in the Gospels. Calvin believed that the Lord's Supper was a real event. But Calvin differed from Luther in teaching that this event happens only *to* believers and *through* their faith. Calvin wrote to a Roman Catholic theologian:

> The presence of Christ, by which we are engrafted into Him, we do not reject from the Supper, nor do we disguise it. We hold that the glorious body of Christ must not be degraded to earthly elements, and there must be no fiction of transubstantiating the bread into Christ and then worshipping it as Christ.

Thus by the middle of the sixteenth century, four views of the Lord's Supper were being taught in Europe:

1. The *Roman Catholics* maintained *transubstantiation*, in which, according to the Fourth Lateran Council of 1215, the substance or material of the bread and wine are changed into the material of Christ's body and blood.

2. For *Luther*, Christ's body and blood were given *together with* the bread and wine, by God's act, not the priest's.

2.3   'In 1549 all the Swiss Reformed Churches adopted Calvin's view of the Lord's Supper, as did the other Reformed Churches of Europe later' (p. 28).
Compare this portrait of Calvin with the one of Luther on p. 8.

3. *Calvin* taught a 'spiritual real presence' of Christ, in which Christ comes only to believers.

4. *Zwingli* and others understood the Lord's Supper as a memorial, a proclamation, and a commitment.

In 1549 all the Swiss Reformed Churches adopted Calvin's view, as did the other Reformed Churches of Europe later. However, many Protestants follow Zwingli's understanding of the Lord's Supper, probably without knowing it.

CALVIN DEFENDS THE REFORMED FAITH

In 1539 Calvin and his associates were expelled from Geneva for a time, because of a disagreement with the city council over Church discipline. At that time one of the ablest Roman Catholic theologians, Cardinal Jacopo Sadoleto, took the occasion to suggest that Geneva should return to its ancient Catholic faith. The Geneva authorities wanted a strong and fitting reply, so they asked Calvin to answer Sadoleto's letter. In spite of his disagreements with the city government, Calvin did reply in September, 1539, giving a good summary of the Reformed faith.

The purpose of the Reformation, Calvin wrote, was not simply to reform errors and abuses in the Church. The real reason for the Reformation was, 'that the light of divine truth has been extinguished, the Word of God buried, the virtue of Christ left in deep darkness, and the office of the minister undermined'. The Reformers intended to 'establish among themselves a better form of the Church'.

Calvin continued that the Church is:

The society of all the saints, spread through all the world and existing in all ages. Yet it is bound together by the doctrine and one spirit of Christ, and it cultivates and observes the unity of faith and brotherly agreement. We deny that we have any disagreement with this Church.

Many groups speak of the Spirit of God, but 'they inevitably tend to sink and bury the Word of God, and make room for their own falsehoods'. The Reformers would return 'to that form which the Apostles instituted. In it we have the only model of the true Church, and whoever deviates from it in the least degree is in error.'

The only unity of the Church is in God Himself. 'Whenever thou (O Lord) didst recommend to us peace and concord, thou didst at the same time show thyself to be the only bond for preserving it.' Continuity with the past is not enough. 'The salvation of man hangs by a thread whose defence turns wholly on his own steady adherence to the religion handed down to him from his forefathers.' This did not mean, however, that Roman Catholics are not also Christians. 'We indeed, Sadoleto, do not deny that those over which you preside are Churches of Christ.' But they were Churches which required reforming according to the Word of God.

Calvin rejected certain Catholic teachings of the Middle Ages, including the necessity of confession to a priest, the intercession of the saints, and the existence of Purgatory. He also defended the Reformation teaching on justification by faith alone. He wrote:

> Wherever the knowledge of it is taken away, the glory of Christ is extinguished, religion abolished, the Church destroyed, and the hope of salvation utterly overthrown ... As all mankind are lost sinners in the sight of God, we hold that Christ is their only righteousness, since by his obedience he has done away with our transgressions, by his sacrifice appeased the divine anger, by his blood washed away our sins, by his cross borne our curse, and by his death made satisfaction for us.

Calvin continued by discussing the Lord's Supper. We have already quoted a passage from this letter (see p. 26). The faith of the Reformation was now being lived and taught in two different ways.

STUDY SUGGESTIONS

WORD STUDY

1. What is the origin of the word 'radical'? What is its meaning as used in this chapter?
2. What does 'transubstantiation' mean? What does this word tell us about the Roman Catholic view of the Lord's Supper?

REVIEW OF CONTENT

3. What are the two basic ideas in Luther's Reformation teaching?
4. What is distinctive about Reformed, as opposed to Lutheran teaching?
5. What basic ideas in Zwingli's thought led to his special teaching on the Lord's Supper?
6. Why may Zwingli be called a 'radical humanist'?
7. What did John Calvin try to do in Geneva?
8. What did the Reformers understand to be the essential characteristics of the Church?
9. In what ways did Luther's teaching on the Lord's Supper differ from that of Roman Catholics?
10. (a) What effect did Zwingli's understanding of the Old Testament have on his view of the Lord's Supper?
    (b) What corrections did Calvin make to Zwingli's view?

11. What, according to Calvin, was the essential purpose of the Reformation?
12. Did Calvin believe Roman Catholics were also Christians? What were his reasons for his view?

DISCUSSION AND RESEARCH

13. How do we find out the meaning of the Word of God?
14. 'Biblical theologians' believe there is one message in the Bible. Do you agree? If so, how would you state it?
15. What does the Bible teach us about what the Church should be like? Give some examples of descriptions of the Church in the Bible, with chapter and verse references. Why has the Church changed since the first century?
16. Do you agree that the Christian life is affected by the customs and circumstances in which the believer lives? If it is, is this a good or a bad thing? In what ways, if any, is a Chinese Methodist different from an American Methodist, or a Tanzanian Lutheran from a German Lutheran, or an Anglican in Kerala from one in London?
17. Do the Gospels give us one way of understanding the Lord's Supper (consider also the 'tradition' that Paul gives in Cor. 11.17–34)? Does it matter if two people come to the Lord's Table with different understandings of what takes place there? What is your own reaction when Church regulations prevent Christians from taking the Lord's Supper together?

CHAPTER 3
Radical Reformers

The division of Christendom in Europe, which began with Martin Luther's condemnation in 1520, proved to be permanent. Protestant and Catholic theologians held a series of conferences to try to settle their differences, the last of which was held in 1541. But they were unsuccessful. Many people hoped that a General Council of the Church would solve the problem, but the meeting of the Council was repeatedly postponed because the Emperor Charles V was at war with the King of France. Religious and political conflicts were always mixed up together in that period. In 1527, soldiers of the Emperor even sacked Rome because the Pope sided with France. The eighteenth century English historian Edward Gibbon commented on this event:

> The ravages of the barbarians whom Alaric led from the banks of the Danube were less destructive than the hostilities exercised by the troops of Charles V, a Catholic prince, who called himself Emperor of the Romans.

Gibbon here compared the event of 1527 with the sack of Rome by Visigoths in 410 which led Augustine to write *The City of God* (see Vol. 1, p. 61).

The Council finally met in 1545, but by that time it was too late to reunite the Church. However, Protestant theologians attended the second session of the Council in 1552, and the religious settlement was eventually achieved by political and military means, when in 1555 the agreement known as the Religious Peace of Augsburg recognized the rights of Lutheran states within the Empire.

But this did not bring matters to a final conclusion. Within France civil war continued from 1562 to 1594, complicated by political quarrels, and reaching a peak of violence when several thousands of Protestants died in the massacres of St Bartholomew's Day in 1572. And a Thirty Years War, mainly between France and the Empire, was fought in the earlier part of the seventeenth century. It was the Peace of Westphalia, also called the Peace of Münster and Osnabruck, from the towns where the treaties were signed in 1648, which settled the religious map of Europe more or less as it is today. According to this settlement:

Northern and Eastern Germany remained Lutheran.

Denmark, Norway, and Sweden, together with their colonies Iceland and Greenland, were made Lutheran by their Kings.

Southern Europe, i.e. Italy, Spain, Portugal, Austria, Southern

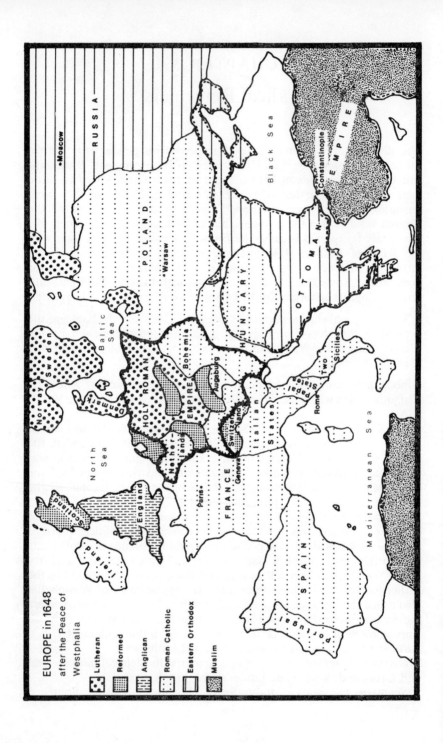

EUROPE in 1648
after the Peace of
Westphalia

Lutheran
Reformed
Anglican
Roman Catholic
Eastern Orthodox
Muslim

RUSSIA

•MOSCOW

POLAND

•Warsaw

Black Sea

Constantinople

OTTOMAN EMPIRE

HUNGARY

Baltic Sea

Sweden

Norway

Denmark

HOLY ROMAN EMPIRE

Bohemia

Augsburg

Nether-land

Switzerland

Italian States

Two Sicilies

•Rome

Papal States

North Sea

Ireland

England

Pueblos

Paris•

FRANCE

Geneva

SPAIN

Portugal

Mediterranean Sea

Germany, and most of France remained Roman Catholic, though the French Huguenots enjoyed nearly 100 years of official toleration under Henry IV's Edict of Nantes, which remained in force from 1598 till 1685.

In the *Netherlands, Scotland, and Switzerland* the Reformed Church was legally established.

The Reformed were also important minorities in France. The Italian Waldensians (see Vol. 2. pp. 152, 153) became Reformed.

England pursued its own course of Reformation (see chapter 4).

Eastern Europe had a more complicated story. Hungary, Czechoslovakia, and Poland remained mainly Roman Catholic, with Orthodox Churches also, and important Reformed, Lutheran, and Radical minorities (see chapter 3).

The Radical Reformation (see below) was illegal everywhere.

The Wars of Religion do not form a happy or enlightening period in Church History. What is important to remember is that the religious divisions of Western Europe followed social and economic divisions, and affected the form which the Churches took. Southern Europe, the heartland of the old Roman Empire, remained Roman Catholic. Broadly speaking, the lands whose languages were based on Latin (called 'Romance' languages, i.e. in 'Roman'-speaking areas, including Italy, France, Southern Switzerland, and Rumania) were faithful to the Roman Church. The German and Scandinavian people were mainly Lutheran. The Reformed were strong in the independent provinces of the Netherlands, where in 1618 the Synod of Dort had settled standards of doctrine for the Dutch Church, and in most of the commercial centres of central and northern Europe. The English, who were always a bit separated from the pressures of the mainland of Europe, went their own way.

REFORMATION FROM BELOW

So far we have studied what scholars call the 'Magisterial' Reformation (from the Latin *magister*, 'master', from which we get 'Master of Arts', M.A., the degree awarded by universities to a learned person). It was a Reformation from the top, led by university-trained scholars, who tried to persuade princes and city councils to reform the Church. We shall see more of this when we study the English Reformation in Chapter Four.

But first we turn to another very important movement, this time a Reformation from below. This Reformation was the work of left-wing or radical reformers, beginning in Luther's Wittenburg and Zwingli's Zürich. In its view of society, the Magisterial Reformation continued the kind of thinking which the Church had known since the time of Constantine (see Vol. 1, pp. 80–82). Most Christians believed that each nation should have only one religion, and that the governments should support the practice of that religion. This is sometimes called 'Constantinian thinking', but it might better be called 'Eusebian thinking', since the thinker who expressed these ideals most clearly was Constantine's admiring biographer, Eusebius of Caesarea (see Vol. 1, p. 81). Eusebius believed that the building of the Church of the Holy Wisdom in Constantinople was what was foretold in Revelation 20, that is, the coming down of the New Jerusalem from heaven.

Out of the turmoil of the Reformation came a strange group of lonely prophets seeking to 'obey God rather than men'. They believed that the way indicated in the New Testament led to a Church of free believers who needed no support or recognition from the government, but only the Word and Spirit of God Himself.

A recent Church historian has called this movement the 'Radical Reformation'. This movement was 'radical' in two ways.

1. The Radical Reformers wanted to apply Luther's ideas in all areas of life in a thoroughgoing way.

2. This movement came at least partly from 'below'. Its leaders were often laymen, working among laymen, and some of them were from the 'roots' of society; peasants and small craftsmen.

Professor George H. Williams, who invented the term 'the Radical Reformation', divides the supporters of this movement into three groups:

1. The first were the *Lutheran Spiritualists*. They were associates of Luther who felt that Luther's emphasis on the Word should be balanced by the effects of the Spirit on believers. Such men as Karlstadt and Müntzer tried to develop a Church which showed in its outward forms the meaning of the liberty of the Spirit which the Gospel proclaims.

2. The next group were the *Anabaptists*. Such men as Conrad Grebel and Balthazar Hübmaier, who were followers of Zwingli in Zürich, believed that the Church must be reconstructed strictly on the basis of imitating Christ's life and such New Testament examples as are given in the early chapters of Acts. They also taught that the Church should be strictly independent from the government.

3. The third group, which we shall study only briefly, Williams calls *Evangelical Rationalists*. They believed that Christian freedom gives every believer the right to re-examine the whole of Christian life and thought on the basis of the Gospel. The one example given here is Miguel Servetus.

TROUBLE AT WITTENBERG

While Luther was hiding in the Wartburg castle, the first signs of division began to appear among his followers. Many of Luther's ordinary lay followers were anxious to show publicly that they had accepted the renewal of the Church which he proclaimed. Among them, Luther's senior colleague, Professor Andreas Karlstadt, took the lead. At Christmas, 1521, Karlstadt made certain changes in the liturgy of the Church. He celebrated mass in ordinary clothes, omitted parts of the Prayer of Consecration, and offered both the bread and the wine to the people. These changes were a revolutionary break from the established traditions of worship. They were similar to those recommended by Wycliffe and the Waldensians (see Vol. 2, chapter 10). The people followed them up by removing the statues from the churches.

Luther was very upset. He saw his theologian's Reformation turning into a people's movement, which conflicted with some of his deepest convictions. No doubt others thought that Luther wanted to do all the reforming himself. In March 1522, Luther left his hiding place and preached every day for a week in Wittenberg, to try and regain control of the Reformation. In his second sermon, on 10 March, he spoke out very plainly:

> The mass is an evil thing, and God is displeased with it, because it is performed as if it were a sacrifice and work of merit. Therefore it must be abolished. Yet Christian love should not employ harshness here, nor force the matter, no one should be dragged away from it by the hair, we should preach the Word, but the results must be left solely to God's good pleasure.
>
> For the Word created heaven and earth and all things; the Word must do this thing, and not we poor sinners.

Relying solely on the Word, Luther quickly took control again. Karlstadt left Wittenberg, and became pastor of a small country church, where he gave up studying theology and put aside his academic gown. He conducted services in the German language, and liked to be called 'Brother Andreas' by his people. Before long, Karlstadt was expelled from Saxony, and moved on to the tolerant city of Basle. The Radical Reformation was carried on by others.

THOMAS MÜNTZER (1488–1525)

The second great Lutheran 'Spiritualist', Thomas Müntzer, pastor at Allstedt in Saxony, understood the work of the Spirit primarily in the social and political movements of the time. Müntzer was not one of Luther's immediate colleagues, but had become a follower of his after hearing the Leipzig Disputation in 1519, when Luther debated the grace of Christ with Dr John Eck. Müntzer went through a troubled personal 'reformation', during which he doubted both the existence of God and the usefulness of the Church. He was influenced by the medieval German mystics, who had emphasized that the Church was primarily a spiritual community.

Müntzer came to believe in a spiritual Church whose members attained the gifts of the Spirit through an intense inner struggle. He felt that Luther offered too quickly the 'sweet Christ' of justification, and passed over the 'bitter Christ' who demands repentance and personal spiritual struggle. Müntzer was acquainted with people of the lower classes, and the peasantry, who resented the injustice caused by the economic changes of the period. Through these associations Müntzer came to believe that the Reformation was a new stage in God's work of liberating the poor and oppressed. He thought of himself as a new Daniel, to whom God had given prophetic insight into the working of history. Müntzer applied the allegory of the statue in the Book of Daniel, Chapter 2, to the feudal order of Europe.

Müntzer expressed these ideas in a powerful sermon which he preached before the rulers of Saxony in July 1524. In this sermon, he expounded the second chapter of Daniel, and began by saying that the Church through most of its history had behaved like an adulteress, who gave herself to the powerful, and turned Christ into a 'harmless scarecrow'. It was to the cruel pagan king Nebuchadnezzar, not to the proud and religious Jews, that God granted a vision of the future. Müntzer claimed that real knowledge of God's revelation is possible only to those who have received the 'inner word' through their own spiritual struggle, which corresponded to Nebuchadnezzar's madness. God gives true understanding, he said, only to those who have been especially set apart as prophets, and who are given an insight which is denied to ordinary scholarly theologians like Luther, 'even if he had eaten through a hundred Bibles'.

Müntzer thought that the Fifth Monarchy of Nebuchadnezzar's vision was European feudalism, whose end was near. 'The poor townspeople and peasants see it more clearly than you do.' What was needed, he said, was a new and violent prophet: 'a new Daniel must arise and interpret to you your vision, and this prophet, as Moses teaches (Deut. 20.2. according to the Latin version) must go in front of the army.' Müntzer probably meant the army of peasants. He insisted that the Reformation must be a political and social movement, and, if necessary, must use force to accomplish God's will in the world:

Beloved, don't give us any old jokes (like Luther!) about how the power of God should do it without your application of the sword . . . the godless person has no right to live when he is in the way of the righteous.

Müntzer ended his sermon with a plea and a threat to the princes:

You cherished Fathers of Saxony, you must hazard all for the sake of the Gospel. In order that this should be done, in a proper and

3.1 The Lutheran 'spiritualist', Thomas Müntzer, 'insisted that the Reformation must be a political and social movement' (p. 36).
He joined the rebelling peasants, was captured, and beheaded—as the engraving shows.

3.2 'The most famous of the Evangelical Rationalists was Miguel Servetus. He believed that the Church must be totally reconstructed' (p. 44).
This eighteenth-century portrait engraving also shows Servetus burnt as a heretic by order of the City Council after Calvin had ordered his arrest.

orderly fashion, our cherished Fathers and Princes should do it. If, however, they do not do it, the sword will be taken from them.

In that case others would become

'The serious servants of God, who execute the wrath of divine wisdom.'

This appeal to the princes for radical social reform was a failure, and Müntzer himself became one of those 'serious servants of God' when he joined the rebelling peasants in August 1524. The Peasants' War did not last long, but it lasted long enough to scare everyone else. The peasants were defeated in May 1525, and Müntzer himself was captured and beheaded.

BAPTISM IN ZÜRICH

The Lutheran Spiritualists felt that Luther had neglected the Spirit in his emphasis on the Word. Meanwhile, in Zürich some of Zwingli's followers came to feel that their leader was not sufficiently obedient to the Word in Scripture. They were concerned, not with the invisible Church of the Spirit, as Luther was, but with recovering the New Testament form of the Church in the sixteenth century.

The actual discussion with Zwingli was over the baptism of babies. The New Testament nowhere says specifically that babies are to be baptized. On the other hand, it repeatedly indicates that baptism is a seal of the faith of those who *already* believe. The formula used in baptism is taken from Jesus's Great Commission (Matt. 28.19, 20), in which Jesus instructs His followers to 'make disciples of all nations, baptizing them'.

Zwingli replied that baptism was the Christian equivalent of the Jewish ceremony of circumcision, though different from circumcision, it is 'made without hands' (Col. 2.11). Baptism is a sign of membership in the Covenant, and as in the Old Testament, the Covenant extends to believers and their children.

Both Zwingli and the Zürich rebels saw clearly where their arguments could lead. If adults only were to be baptized, then the Church would consist only of true believers. It would no longer consist of *all* the citizens of the city or country. The Church would become a 'free' Church, supported by its members, and not directly responsible to the government. If Church-membership and citizenship were no longer identical, then the tie which had bound the Church to the government since Constantine's time would be broken. Kings would no longer rule 'by the grace of God', and pastors would no longer be required to preach obedience to the rulers.

In January 1525, the City Council of Zürich arranged a debate between Zwingli and Conrad Grebel, Felix Manz, and Balthazar Hübmaier on the subject of baptism. They voted that Zwingli had won, and ordered all babies in the Canton to be presented for baptism. Three days later the rebels held a sort of revival meeting outside Zürich, in which Conrad Grebel was baptized, and in turn baptized others. From this event the rebels came to be known as 'Anabaptists', that is 'the again-baptized' or 'rebaptized', because, of course, they had all been baptized before as babies.

This action horrified Christian Europe, Protestant and Catholic alike. Not only was the Eusebian way of thinking (see p. 34) rejected, but the validity of infant baptism which all had received was denied. People might ask, as the disciples asked Jesus, 'Who then can be saved?'

The official reaction was quick. Grebel died in prison, Manz was drowned—because he liked water so well, Hübmaier was burned at the stake. There are official records of the execution of many hundreds of Anabaptists during the Reformation period. The Religious Peace of Augsburg recognized the rights of Lutherans, and the Peace of West-phalia did the same for the Reformed, but the Anabaptists never had any legal status until the eighteenth century. However, the Anabaptists suffered and survived. They gloried in martyrdom, and published a book about it which they called *Martyrs' Mirror*. They might have applied to themselves one of Luther's marks of the true Church: 'the holy bearing of the Holy Cross'.

Anabaptists were tolerated at various times in parts of Southern Germany, in Eastern Europe, and especially in the Netherlands. Later they were invited to become farmers in Poland and Russia, and in the nineteenth and twentieth centuries many emigrated to the Americas.

THE FAITH OF THE ANABAPTISTS

The Anabaptists agreed strongly with Luther that everyone must believe for himself. That was the basic reason why they rejected infant baptism. At the same time they were very good 'Churchmen'. That is, they believed that the first duty of every Christian is to be a loyal member of his local congregation, and subject to its discipline. More than any other Christian group they used excommunication as a means of discipline, on the basis of Matthew 18.15–18. They believed that every congregation must be completely united, both in belief and in way of life. Every congregation determined its own statement of faith, its own form of government, and its own order of worship. And yet there is a remarkable continuity in belief and practice from the Zürich radicals to the twentieth-century Anabaptists.

The clearest statement of Anabaptists' principles is also the earliest,

39

known as the 'Schleitheim Confession' (1527). This statement was sent to Zwingli, who attacked its teachings, and so did Calvin later on.

The seven points made in the Schleitheim Confession are:

1. *Baptism:* 'Baptism shall be given to all who have learned repentance and amendment of life. This excludes infant baptism, the highest and chief abomination of the Pope.'

2. *Excommunication:* 'The ban shall be employed with all those who have given themselves to the Lord.'

The Anabaptists were serious about their faith and life. They believed that the free Church must be free to decide who is and who is not a faithful disciple of Christ.

3. *The Lord's Supper:* 'All those who wish to break one bread in rememberance of the broken body of Christ ... shall be united beforehand by baptism in one body of Christ, which is the Church of God.'

Christian fellowship, founded on faith, precedes participation in the sacraments. Many Anabaptist groups practise 'close communion.' This means that only the members in good standing of one congregation may take communion together. This statement indicates also that the Anabaptists preserved Zwingli's teaching that the Lord's Supper is a 'remembering' of what Christ has done for us.

4. *Separation from the World:* 'A separation shall be made from the evil and from the wickedness which the devil planted in the world; in this manner, simply that we shall not have fellowship with them and not run with them in the multitude of their abominations.'

One way in which the Anabaptists practised this 'separation' was in marriage. There was true equality of men and women in their congregation, with both husbands and wives as full, believing Church-members. For this reason, to the scandal of Christian Europe, some approved of divorce and remarriage on the basis of Paul's teaching, 'Do not be mismated with unbelievers' (2 Cor. 6.14). Thus Anabaptists were free to leave their Catholic or Protestant spouses in order to marry other Anabaptists. Later, some groups also 'separated' themselves by distinctive clothing.

5. *The Office of the Minister:* 'This office shall be to read, to admonish, and to teach, to discipline, to lead out in prayer ... to lift up the bread when it is broken. This one, moreover, shall be supported by the Church which has chosen him.'

Already at this early time there was an official ministry of the Anabaptist Church. Ministers supported themselves and received offerings from the congregation, rather than being paid by the government out of taxes. They were elected by the congregation itself, rather than being appointed by a bishop or Church board.

6. *Of the Sword:* 'The sword is ordained by God outside the per-

3.3 'The Anabaptists were very good "Churchmen". . . . There was true equality of men and women in the congregation' (pp. 39, 40).

This engraving of Anabaptists at the Lord's Supper seems to show more women than men.

fection of Christ.' According to this teaching, Paul's insistence on the right of rulers to use force applies only to unbelievers, not to believers. 'In the perfection of Christ, however, only the ban is used for a warning and for the excommunication of one who has sinned, without putting the flesh to death.'

Since Constantine's time, Christian Europe had accepted the idea that religious offences were also civil offences, and should be punished by the government. In fact, religious offences were the most serious of all, because they threatened the unity of the nation or Empire. Perhaps behind this deep conviction lay the pre-Christian idea that religious obedience was the foundation of the success and prosperity of the people. Anabaptists also held that Christians should never sue anyone in court. Of course, they were often brought to court by others!

> 'Shall one be a magistrate if one is chosen as such? The answer is as follows: They wished to make Christ a king, but he fled and did not view it as the arrangement of his Father. Thus shall we do as he did, and follow him, and so we shall not walk in darkness.'

If Christians are not to go to court or approve the death sentence, it follows that they must also not be responsible for courts, executioners, or soldiers. In practice, Anabaptists did not take part in government at all. Even today some of the stricter Anabaptist groups do not vote in elections. Separation from the world was understood especially as separation from active involvement in government.

7. *The Swearing of Oaths:* Christ, who teaches the perfection of the Law, prohibits all swearing to His followers . . . it is for this reason that all swearing is forbidden: we cannot fulfill that which we promise when we swear, for we cannot change the least thing in us.

Anabaptists refused to take an oath of allegiance, or swear to tell the truth in court. They could testify to the mightiness of God, but they would not make promises in His name which they might or might not be able to fulfill. From the point of view of the government, this was one of the most suspicious of all Anabaptist teachings. In the free cities all citizens were required to swear an oath of allegiance every year. Right from the start, the three basic principles of what one of their historians has called 'the Anabaptist Vision' have been clear:

(a) The Christian life as brotherhood,
(b) The overwhelming importance of obedience to Christ,
(c) Separation from the world.

We have seen there is very little theology in this Confession of faith. That is as it should be. Anabaptists understood the Christian life as very simple and practical. The whole of the Christian faith and life were summed up in Jesus's call: 'Follow me.'

CATASTROPHE AT MÜNSTER

Among the sixteenth-century Anabaptists, there were a small minority who added to the faith of Schleitheim the belief in the near return of Christ. Melchior Hoffmann, the Anabaptist teacher of Strasbourg, believed that Christ would return in 1535, and then the final battle of the world would take place. Hoffmann himself was in prison in 1535, and died there in 1543, but his teachings influenced some Anabaptists both in Germany and the Netherlands. Theologians describe this kind of teaching as 'apocalyptic', since it sounds like and is influenced by the Book of Revelation, also called the Apocalypse. According to apocalyptic teaching, the world is getting worse and worse, not better and better, and the worse it gets, the nearer is God's judgement day. Thus, as their situation became more desperate, the Hoffmannite Anabaptists became more hopeful and more militant.

At the beginning of 1534, the German free city of Münster, whose ruler was an archbishop, found itself in the extraordinary situation of having as its chief pastor a man who supported Anabaptist teachings. News of this surprising development led many oppressed Anabaptists to move to Münster to enjoy the 'peace of Zion' there. An Anabaptist majority came to dominate the city council. The Hoffmannite leader from the Netherlands, Jan Mathijs, believed the 'conversion' of Münster to be a sign of the end of the world. Many other Christians probably agreed with him in this.

In February the archbishop's troops beseiged Münster, and Jan Mathijs ordered all who refused rebaptism to leave the city. The siege of Münster lasted fifteen months. The citizens depended on reinforcements from the Netherlands which never came, and most of the inhabitants were killed when the city fell.

Both Catholics and Protestants took the events of Münster as proof that Anabaptist teachings led to immorality and bloodshed. Anabaptists were hunted everywhere, but they were gradually reorganized by a former priest named Menno Simons, who became the Elder of the Dutch Anabaptists. He began secret visitations of Anabaptist groups in 1536, refuting the errors of Hoffmannite apocalypticism and insisting that the Anabaptists give the Christian witness of peaceful living. An important group of Anabaptists today call themselves 'Mennonites' in honour of his work.

SERVETUS AND THE EVANGELICAL RATIONALISTS

The Evangelical Rationalists, as they are called by Professor Williams, did not resemble either the Anabaptists or the Müntzerites very much, although their ideas had something in common with those of Andreas

43

Karlstadt. They were not an organized movement, but rather a group of individualistic thinkers, including a number of Catholics from Spain and Italy. Their followers formed continuing Churches only in Hungary and Poland, but their thought has influenced individual Christian thinkers of later periods who often refer to themselves as 'liberal Christians'. These thinkers have often combined mystical religion with a deep interest in philosophy.

The most famous of all the Evangelical Rationalists was a Spanish physician named *Miguel Servetus*. Servetus led a very adventurous life, often living under a false name, and was hunted by all Reformation groups. His most important idea was that it was not enough to *reform* the Church: the Church must be totally *reconstructed*. He expressed this idea in the title of his major theological book, which is, in Latin *Restitutio Christianismi*, published in 1553. The title is intended to make fun of Calvin's major work, called in Latin the *Institutio*. In addition to being a pun, the title points to Servetus's main idea: the Church must be 'restituted'; i.e. reconstituted or restructured, there must be a second and much more radical Reformation. The true form of the Church had been lost long ago, he thought. So it was necessary to start all over again, using the Bible, the light of the Spirit, and man's reason, as guides.

Servetus was brave enough (or foolish enough) to send a copy of the *Restitutio* to Calvin for his comments. Calvin did indeed comment, and also called for Servetus's arrest as a heretic. Servetus attended Calvin's preaching one Sunday in Geneva. Calvin recognized him, he was arrested, and burned to death, the only heretic to die in Geneva.

THE RADICAL REFORMERS' CONTINUING INFLUENCE

When we study the Magisterial Reformation, we learn about the origin of the major Protestant bodies today: Lutheran, Reformed, and Anglican. The contribution of the Radical Reformation is quite different. Church bodies which originated in the Radical Reformation have never been large or influential. What is important is the continuing influence of their ideas. Most Christians today accept such 'Radical' ideas as the belief in the Church as a free association. Very few Christians today believe that the stake and the torture chamber are the proper place to discuss theology. Perhaps most important of all, the Radicals of the sixteenth century set an example of free, honest, and sharp questioning of traditional Christian ideas.

Some of the more important continuing ideas of the Radical Reformation are:

1. *The Free Church:* The Church was understood to be a free

association of believers. The Church is and must be free in three ways:

(a) *Free in membership.* The Church consists of those who freely choose to follow Jesus Christ.

(b) *Free in faith and government.* The Church must decide its own form and its own faith. This can be done at the level of the local congregation, or at the level of higher associations of Churches.

(c) The Church must demand *religious freedom.* If the Church is composed of members who freely choose to follow Jesus Christ, then the Church itself must demand the right for people of all religious bodies and forms of belief to practise their faith and to persuade others.

2. *The Connection between Faith and Life:* All Christians, of course, believe that faith and life are related. Lutherans, the Reformed, and Roman Catholics all have their own typical ways of expressing this. The Radical Reformation, however, made this a major matter of faith. Jesus was to be followed, and the chief element in the Christian life was discipleship. Other branches of the faith disagree with this emphasis, but the fact remains that the Anabaptists, taking the Sermon on the Mount as the New Christian Law, made major discoveries concerning the possibilities of the life of love and of the renewing of society by a radical witness.

3. *The Suffering Witness:* We can compare the different families of the Reformation by saying that Luther saw Christ primarily as the *high priest*, reconciling man to God; Calvin saw Him as the *king*, the only ruler of the Church and the world; while the Radicals saw Him as *prophet*, speaking against the darkness of the world. The Radicals saw the Church as against the world, and Christians as a minority in the world. The truest Christian witness, they believed, was the witness of suffering. Christians who truly follow the Lamb of God must be prepared to be made a sacrifice, as He was.

4. *A Hopeful Theology:* Many Christians today are interested in what is called the Theology of Hope. The 'hope' on which this theology is based is the hope that God is still busy in this world, making it a fit place for His children to live in. When they speak of 'discerning the hand of God in history', they are using the kind of thinking that comes from that strange 'prophet in front of the army', Thomas Müntzer. Both Christian theologians and Marxist philosophers are interested in the ideas of that tragic thinker today.

CHANGING WAYS OF WORSHIP

The most obvious changes in Church life brought about by the Reformation were in matters of worship. But these changes came into the Protestant Churches only gradually. At the beginning, the leaders of the Reformation were mainly interested in questions of doctrine and

Church organization. But within a few years, changes of that sort led to reforms of worship as well.

Reforms in worship ranged widely from conservative to radical. The earliest changes were made by the followers of Luther, in response to ideas expressed in some of his writings. As early as 1521, people who were influenced by him celebrated a mass in Wittenberg using the German language instead of Latin, and giving the lay people the consecrated wine as well as the bread. In 1522 and 1523, other Churches in Germany tried out similar reforms.

Basically *Luther* was conservative about changes in the liturgy. He believed that the Bible should provide the standard by which to judge how Christians should worship. But he believed that if a practice was not forbidden by the Bible, it could be retained. For this reason he wanted to continue to use traditional forms of worship, but to purify them of what he felt were beliefs contrary to the Bible. Above all, he wanted to do away with anything which suggested that Church people could use the mass as a way of obtaining God's grace by repeating in it Christ's sacrifice on the cross.

Because Luther feared that his followers were going too far in their reforms of worship, he decided that he must make clear his own position. He did this in 1523, in a work called the *Formula Missae* (Latin: Form of the Mass). Since many regarded this statement as too conservative, in 1525 he pushed his reforms further in a second publication called the *Deutsche Messe* (German: The German Mass).

Meanwhile, in Zürich in Switzerland, *Ulrich Zwingli* took a more radical position (see p. 21). He wanted to do away with what he felt was the irrational confusion in medieval beliefs about the relationship between spirit and matter in the sacraments. Since God is Spirit, it seemed clear to Zwingli that God must use spiritual rather than material ways to communicate His grace to people. As Zwingli understood it, these spiritual means were to be found in the reading and preaching of the Word of God.

Under Zwingli's influence, the preaching service became the normal Sunday service, and the Lord's Supper became a special service to be used only four times a year.

Another Reformation leader, *Martin Bucer*, had been influenced by both Luther and Zwingli. During his ministry in the German city of Strasbourg, he worked for a form of worship that would provide a middle way between Luther's conservative reforms and Zwingli's radical changes. The order of service which Bucer developed was more conservative than that of Zwingli, but the wording of its prayers moved farther from traditional usage than the Lutheran forms did. In Strasbourg, the Lord's Supper was celebrated every week at the cathedral, and once a month in the parish churches.

The worship of Strasbourg is important chiefly because of its influence on *John Calvin*. Calvin spent most of his ministry in Geneva, but from 1538 until 1541 he worked with the French-speaking congregation in Strasbourg, and became familiar with the form of worship used there. He was impressed by it, and when he returned to Geneva, he began using a French translation of the service, with some changes of his own. From Geneva, different versions of this service spread widely among Reformed Churches all over Europe.

In his attitude towards the Bible as a standard for worship, Calvin was more conservative than Luther. In order to be true to the New Testament tradition, he felt it necessary to discard many of the liturgical practices that had grown up through the centuries. For this reason, the Reformed Churches moved further away from the Catholic heritage of the Middle Ages in their worship than the Lutheran Churches did.

Throughout his ministry, John Calvin believed strongly that to be true to the New Testament tradition, the weekly Sunday service must be the Lord's Supper. But before he arrived in Geneva, the people there, under Zwinglian influence, had already accepted the custom of celebrating the Lord's Supper only four times a year. Despite his best efforts, Calvin could not pursuade the authorities to change this practice. Thus despite Calvin's objections, infrequent Communion became customary for Calvinist Churches.

For many years after the Reformation, nearly all Protestant denominations used set liturgical forms for Sunday worship. But some smaller groups turned away from this practice. They believed that each congregation should be free to order its own forms of worship, and that instead of reading prayers from a book, the minister should lead prayer in his own words. Of those who held this position, the best known were the Anabaptists (see pp. 39, 40). To begin with, the larger Protestant denominations rejected this kind of worship. But in later centuries, except for the Lutherans, Protestants on the Continent of Europe accepted a free form of worship for their normal Sunday services. For special services, however, most of these denominations still continued to use certain set forms.

STUDY SUGGESTIONS

WORD STUDY

1. What is the meaning of the word 'Anabaptist'?
2. Some Anabaptists and other groups practise 'close communion'. What does that mean?
3. Where does the word 'apocalyptic' come from? Give an example of an apocalyptic teaching.
4. From where do the 'Mennonites' get their name?

REVIEW OF CONTENT

5. What was 'radical' about the Radical Reformation?
6. What was the 'trouble at Wittenberg'?
7. What did Thomas Müntzer disagree with in Luther's teaching?
8. How did Müntzer understand the 'Fifth Monarchy' in Daniel 2?
9. (a) Why did some Christians come to doubt that the baptism of babies was right?
   (b) Why did the Magisterial Reformers fear the rejection of baptism of babies?
10. What was the *Martyrs' Mirror*?
11. List some special teachings of the Anabaptists about the Church?
12. Why did the Anabaptists approve of divorce?
13. Why would Anabaptists not hold office in government?
14. What 'Hoffmannite' ideas led to the 'Catastrophe at Münster'?
15. What was the most important teaching of Miguel Servetus?
16. What teachings of the Radical Reformation continue to influence all branches of the Church today?
17. Why did Luther decide it was necessary for him to publish a new version of the mass in German?
18. Why did Zwingli disagree with Luther's ideas on the proper form of Protestant worship?
19. In what ways did Calvin's understanding of worship differ from Zwingli's and Luther's?

DISCUSSION AND RESEARCH

20. The Magisterial Reformers felt that the Roman Catholics paid too much attention to the teachings of the Fathers and the Popes, and not enough to those of the Bible. They also felt that the Radicals were more concerned about their own spiritual experiences, than with the text of the Bible. In interpreting a text from the Bible, which do you consider to be the most important:
   (a) What the biblical scholars say that it means,
   (b) How it is interpreted in your own Church, or
   (c) The way it speaks to you in your present circumstances?
21. Can the meaning of a Bible passage ever change? Does God reveal new things that are not mentioned in the Bible? Give examples to support your answer.
22. Since the coming of Jesus Christ, does all of God's saving work take place through the Church, or is God still doing things 'by Himself' in the world? Could a new Cyrus (Isa. 44, 45) arise, i.e. a political leader who serves God without knowing it? Have there been any since Cyrus? Does God sometimes do things in spite of the Church?
23. What is the difference between the 'reformation' and the 'restitution'

of the Church? Is it possible that the true Church might disappear entirely, and reappear at a later time? Do you know any Churches today who hold this belief? Give examples.

24. Does the government in your country support the Church? If so, do you think this is a good arrangement? Should Church people always obey the laws of their rightful government?

25. What is your opinion about capital punishment (i.e. being put to death for breaking the law)?

26. Should Christians take part in war? All kinds of wars?

27. Calvin 'felt it necessary to discard certain liturgical practices that had grown up through the centuries' (p. 47). What effect does it have on worshippers, when familiar forms of worship are discarded? Which groups in a congregation are most likely to welcome liturgical changes and which are most likely to oppose them? What reasons are the different groups likely to give for their reactions to change?

CHAPTER 4

Reformation in England

The Reformation of the Church in England was quite different from the Reformation in Continental Europe. England is an island nation, which has always been somewhat separated from the affairs of the nations of continental Europe. In the sixteenth century the government became more centralized, and people's national feelings were stronger in England than elsewhere. The history of England during this period was strongly influenced by the character of its monarchs. In 1485 a long series of bitter and destructive civil wars came to an end. Four important events at this time greatly affected English life.

1. The weak rule of the medieval Plantagenet kings came to an end, being replaced by the strong and energetic House of Tudor.

2. England lost all its possessions in France, which gave it more time to devote to internal affairs.

3. The civil wars had nearly eliminated the old feudal nobility, giving the monarchs a free hand to centralize the country.

4. England began manufacturing its own woollen cloth, rather than shipping the wool to Europe.

It was in this period, too, that the island nation became a great sea power. Her sailors raided Spanish shipping from the Americas. They found a northern sea-passage to Russia, and sailed around the world. In 1600 the British East India Company was chartered. A darker side of this international commerce had shown itself when John Hawkins began the slave trade, bringing Africans from Guinea to Europe, in 1562.

During the sixteenth century, England and Scotland were separate nations. The Reformation in Scotland was quite different from that in England, and did not produce a new branch of the Church as the English Reformation did. The Scottish Reformation will be dealt with later in this chapter (see p. 65).

KING HENRY TAKES A NEW WIFE

The idea of a Reformation of the Church was not a new one in England. One of the earliest of the 'Reformers before the Reformation' was the Oxford professor, John Wycliffe (see Vol. 2, p. 156), and one of the most radical of the advocates of a General Council as the supreme authority in the Church was another Englishman, William of Ockham. In 1526, after going to visit Luther, William Tyndale published an unauthorized English version of the New Testament. Copies were

4.1 King Henry VIII—'single and supreme lord' of the Church in England (p. 52).
Holbein's portrait sketch shows Henry's stubborn character.

seized and burned, and Tyndale himself died for his faith ten years later. Later an English version of the whole Bible was published by Miles Coverdale.

However, England's kings kept the country loyal to the Catholic faith and the Roman Church. King John had accepted his crown from the Pope in 1215, and, as we have already learned (see p. 11), the second Tudor monarch, Henry VIII, actually wrote a book replying to Luther's *Babylonian Captivity*. Like the other European rulers, however, the Tudors wanted to rule their own land without help from the Pope.

Although in many ways England followed its own course, the Tudors continued to be involved in the politics of continental Europe. This was because of the custom that kings should marry women of royal or noble blood, often the daughters of other kings. Henry VIII married a Spanish princess, Catherine of Aragon, who was the aunt of the most powerful ruler in Europe, the Emperor Charles V. Queen Catherine had formerly been married to Henry's older brother Arthur, who died before becoming king. Catherine bore a number of children to Henry, but all died young except a daughter, Mary, who was never physically strong. Henry feared he would never have a son. Also, he was attracted to a lady of the court, Anne Boleyn. He came to doubt that his marriage was valid, since it was illegal for a man to marry his brother's widow, though the Pope had given special dispensation for the marriage at the time.

Henry asked his Chancellor, Thomas Wolsey, Cardinal Archbishop of York, to arrange for his marriage to be annulled, or declared invalid. Cardinal Wolsey failed in this. An annulment had to come from the Pope, Clement VII, who was afraid to make an enemy of Emperor Charles by humiliating his aunt. A theologian at Cambridge University, Thomas Cranmer, suggested that the universities of Europe should be asked for their advice. The replies mostly favoured the annulment, but the Pope would not change his mind. Henry then took things into his own hands. He made the English clergy declare him to be the 'single and supreme lord' of the Church in England. By then Cranmer had become Archbishop of Canterbury, and Primate (head) of the Church in England. Cranmer declared Henry's marriage to Catherine annulled, and married him to Anne Boleyn in 1533. The next year Parliament regularized the situation by passing the Act of Supremacy, which declared that the king was 'the only supreme head in earth of the Church of England'—and thus no longer under the Pope's jurisdiction.

This left the English in the strange position of being a Catholic Church which rejected the authority of the Pope. Not everyone took this change lightly, and in 1535 a number of Englishmen died for their loyalty to the Pope, including Thomas More, who succeeded Wolsey as Lord Chancellor.

FOUR THOMASES

The sixteenth century was a very eventful period in English history. It may be helpful to look at a few of the men who helped to bring about the startling religious changes which took place during this period. We divide them into the Catholic 'right', the King's men, and the Reformed 'left'.

The most eminent Catholic of the period was the Lord Chancellor, *Sir Thomas More*. He had studied classics at Oxford, and considered entering the priesthood, but became a lawyer instead. He was a friend of the great humanist Erasmus, and of the English biblical scholar, John Colet. Like Erasmus, More was a wise critic of the failures of the European peoples of his day. He wrote a book called *Utopia*, from a Greek word which means 'the good place'. The book became famous, and its title became a common English word. In it, More contrasted the way the world is, with the way it could be.

More became a member of Parliament, but continued to be interested in theology. In 1523 he answered Luther's reply to Henry VIII's book on the sacraments. More succeeded Cardinal Wolsey as Lord Chancellor in 1529. He was a strong supporter of the king, and upheld the rights of the English nation, yet he remained a good Catholic. He resigned as Chancellor in 1532 over the question of Henry's divorce, and refused to promise allegiance to Henry's daughter by Anne Boleyn, if she should become queen. As a result he was imprisoned in the Tower of London for over a year. He spent the time writing a *Dialogue of Comfort Against Tribulation*. In 1535 he suffered what Shakespeare called 'the long divorce of steel', when he was beheaded for his loyalty to the Pope. Just four hundred years later another Pope declared him a saint.

The most noted of the 'King's men' was *Thomas, Cardinal Wolsey*. He came from a middle-class family, and rose to great eminence in the Church, but lost favour for being too ambitious, and too unscrupulous in his use of power. In 1514 Wolsey became Archbishop of York, the second bishop in England, and Lord Chancellor, the head of the English legal system and president of the House of Lords. In the same year he was made a Cardinal. He seems to have wanted to become Pope, and his ambitions and his unsuccessful attempt to arrange the annulment of King Henry's marriage led to his disgrace. He was charged with high treason, but died on the way to his trial in 1530.

Wolsey's very able associate, and successor as adviser to the King was *Thomas Cromwell*, who was chiefly responsible for the suppression of the English monasteries. By 1540 there were no monasteries left in England. Their riches went into the royal treasury, and their lands and buildings were given to favoured noblemen. This was an important

4.2 Sir Thomas More—'the most eminent catholic of the period' (p. 53) seated, centre, as sketched by Holbein with members of his family.

reason for the support which the English nobility gave to the Reformation. Some of the great houses belonging to noble families in England still bear their original name of 'abbey' or priory'. Before this suppression, one third of England's land was owned by the Church. Cromwell, like Wolsey, fell from favour over a royal marriage. Henry's third Queen, Jane Seymour, who succeeded Anne Boleyn, died giving birth to the future king, Edward VI. Cromwell's candidate to succeed her was unacceptable to Henry, and Cromwell was charged with treason, lost his position, and his life.

The leader of the Protestants in the English Reformation was our fourth Thomas, *Thomas Cranmer*, Archbishop of Canterbury. Cranmer was a gentle scholar and a man of faith. It was his misfortune that he believed strongly in the right of the government to decide the form of the national religion. He tried to maintain these principles while serving three Tudor monarchs as Primate of England. He annulled three of Henry's marriages, and married him twice. Cranmer was sincerely devoted to the Reformed faith, and he himself married a niece of the great Lutheran theologian Andreas Osiander. But Cranmer's greatest contribution to the English Church was not as a theologian or Church administrator. He was the chief author of the first two editions of the Book of Common Prayer, the English Liturgy of the Church of England. Cranmer's liturgical English has influenced the English language ever since. We will return to his later career in the following section.

PROTESTANTISM AND REACTION: 1547–1558

As we have already seen, the religious situation in England was very much influenced by the reigning monarch. Henry VIII insisted on the complete governmental independence of the Church of England, but also kept it strictly to the Catholic faith. On one hand he abolished the monasteries, and ordered an English Bible to be placed in each church. On the other hand, over Cranmer's objections, he persuaded Parliament to pass the Six Articles of 1539. These articles reaffirmed Catholic teaching on transubstantiation, the withholding of the wine from the laity at the Lord's Supper, the celibacy of the clergy, the validity of the vows of the monks, and the right to hold private masses without the presence of a congregation. The Protestant writer John Foxe referred to the Six Articles as 'the whip of six strings'. Two bishops resigned because of the Articles, but Cranmer, true to his principle of obedience to the king, accepted the Articles, and sent his own wife away.

But when Henry died in 1547 he was succeeded by the nine-year-old Edward VI, whose guardian was a convinced Protestant. During the six years of Edward's short reign the Six Articles were repealed, and

Cranmer was free to begin the reformation of the Church. He published two editions of the Book of Common Prayer, in 1549 and 1552, which enforced a thoroughly Reformed pattern of worship in the English Church. The service was simple, and so were the garments of the priest. Ceremonies were reduced to a minimum, and great emphasis was placed on the reading of the Bible.

The steady movement towards a radically Protestant theology is shown by an important change made between the first and second prayer books. In the Communion Service of 1549, the priest is directed to say, when he administers the bread and wine: 'The body of our Lord Jesus Christ which is shed for thee, preserve thy body and soul unto everlasting life', and 'the blood of our Lord Jesus Christ which was shed for thee, preserve thy body and soul unto everlasting life'. In the service of 1552, the priest was instructed to say instead: 'take and eat this, in remembrance that Christ died for thee, and feed on him in thy heart with thanksgiving', and 'Drink this in remembrance that Christ's blood was shed for thee, and be thankful.'

Scholars differ in their interpretation of Cranmer's theological ideas about the sacraments. But the change we have noted shows that he was prepared to write words which could be understood in a Zwinglian way (see p. 28). According to the 1552 version, the Christian 'feeds on' Christ in his 'heart by faith', and does not actually eat the actual body of Christ, furthermore, the Lord's Supper is offered 'in remembrance' of what Christ *has* done, in the past. Most Anglicans later came to reject the Zwinglian implications of these words.

Edward VI, who never married, died of tuberculosis in 1553, at the age of 16. The Protector, the Duke of Northumberland, feared to lose his life if Edward's logical successor, Henry VIII's eldest daughter, Mary, should succeed to the throne, as she was daughter of the Spanish Catholic Catherine of Aragon. So he persuaded the dying Edward to designate a young cousin, Lady Jane Grey, as his successor. Lady Jane, granddaughter of a sister of Henry VIII, was fourteen years old. Northumberland married her to his son, hoping, as a result, to remain at the head of the English government.

The plot failed, and the hopes of the Reformed Protestants in England died with Edward. Lady Jane was officially queen for nine days, but England's leaders rejected this irregular succession, and after the Lord Mayor of London declared himself for Mary, the desperate attempt collapsed. Lady Jane Grey was condemned to death, and two years later, after a revolt against Mary which involved her father, was beheaded. But this tragic girl lived long enough to confess her faith most strikingly, showing herself a clear witness to the Reformed faith of Edward's and Cranmer's day in England. The sixteen-year-old ex-queen recorded her interview with the Catholic prison chaplain four days before her execution, in *A certain communication between Lady Jane and Master Feckenham, four days before her death, even word for word, her own hand being put thereto'*. On the subject of justification she says:

> *Feckenham:* Is there nothing else required in a Christian but to believe in God?
>
> *Jane:* Yes, we must believe in Him, we must love Him with all our heart, with all our soul and all our mind, and our neighbour as ourself.
>
> *Feckenham:* Why then faith justifies not, nor saves not.
>
> *Jane:* Yes, truly faith (as St Paul says) alone justifies.
>
> *Feckenham:* Why St Paul says: If I have all faith without love it is nothing.
>
> *Jane:* True it is, for how can I love him in whom I trust not? Or how can I trust him whom I love not? Faith and love agree together, and yet love is comprehended in faith.
>
> *Feckenham:* How shall we love our neighbour?
>
> *Jane:* To love our neighbour is to feed the hungry, clothe the naked, and give drink to the thirsty, and to do to him as we would do to ourselves.
>
> *Feckenham:* Why then is it necessary to salvation to do good works and it is not sufficient to believe?
>
> *Jane:* I deny that and I affirm that faith alone saves. But it is fitting for Christians in token that they follow their master Christ, to do good works, yet may we not say that they profit to salvation.

Thus the young condemned girl gives us one of the simplest and clearest statements of Luther's teaching on justification by faith alone. They then turn to the sacraments, and Lady Jane affirms Zwingli's understanding of the Lord's Supper.

> *Jane:* The sacrament of the Lord's Supper is offered unto me as a sure seal and testimony that I am by the blood of Christ, which He shed for me on the Cross, made partaker of the everlasting kingdom.
>
> *Feckenham:* Why, does Christ speak these words: Take, eat, this is my body? Require we any plainer words?
>
> *Jane:* I grant He says so, and He says: I am the vine, I am the door, but yet He is never more the vine nor door ... God forbid that I should say that I eat the very natural body and blood of Christ.
>
> *Feckenham:* Why is it not possible that Christ by his power could make his body both to be eaten and broken, as to be born of a woman without the seed of a man, and as to walk on the sea, having

a body, and other such like miracles as He wrought by His power only?

Jane: Yes, truly, if God would have done at His supper a miracle, He might have done so; but I say He intended no work or miracle, but only to break His body and shed His blood on the Cross for our sins.

The Lord's Supper is not a new miracle, but the vivid reminder to God's people that the foundation for their new life is the death of their Lord.

Mary was raised a Catholic, and married the most ardently Catholic ruler of the sixteenth century, Philip II of Spain. Mary was never strong, and the English people, who disapproved of her Spanish marriage, had no great affection for her. Her short and unhappy reign lasted only five years, but during those years she managed to convince the people that they never wanted another Catholic ruler.

Mary, naturally, resented the fact that her mother's marriage to Henry VIII had been declared illegal and sinful. With the help of Cardinal Reginal Pole, who eventually succeeded Cranmer as Primate of England, she revoked all the changes which had been made in the English Church since 1529, except for the dissolution of the monasteries. On All Saints Day, 1554, Cardinal Pole declared that England was absolved from heresy. Many Churchmen, of course, resisted this, and nearly three hundred people, including three bishops, were executed during Mary's reign. Thomas Cranmer went through an intense struggle between his Reformed faith and his principles of obedience to the monarch. His final loyalty was to the Reformation, and he was burned to death on 21 March 1556. The most vivid picture we have of this period is a very Protestant one, a kind of English *Martyrs' Mirror*, in a book entitled *Acts and Monuments*, by John Foxe, commonly known as 'Foxe's Book of Martyrs'.

ESTABLISHMENT OF THE CHURCH OF ENGLAND
1558–1603

As Mary Tudor left no heir, she was succeeded by her younger half-sister, Elizabeth, daughter of Anne Boleyn. Elizabeth kept her personal religious convictions to herself, but her upbringing was Protestant, and her legitimacy depended upon the acts which established the Church of England, also known as the 'Anglican' Church. Elizabeth's succession was never recognized by the Pope, nor by Spain, since Philip II was unhappy at losing his power over England. In 1588 Spain sent a great fleet, known as the Invincible Armada, in an unsuccessful attempt to conquer England. Throughout her reign, Elizabeth was subject to plots to overthrow her. This of course, hardened the anti-Catholic feelings of the English, since Elizabeth was a very popular queen.

The Elizabethan period in England was the time of the nation's greatest cultural achievements. It could be called the 'English renaissance'. Her explorers literally sailed around the world, and her musicians, philosophers, poets, and playwrights were the greatest in Europe of the time. Best-known of all was the playwright and poet William Shakespeare. Shakespeare, like his queen, was officially a Protestant, but his humanity was much too broad to be limited by religious divisions.

Quite early in Elizabeth's reign the Church of England was established upon a permanent basis. In 1559 Parliament proclaimed the queen to be 'Supreme Governor of the Church in England'. It was thought that 'governor' was more appropriate than 'head' for a woman, since the Apostle Paul believed the man was head over the woman. But all English monarchs since that time have contented themselves with being 'Governor' of the Anglican Church. The Second Act of Supremacy declared that the orthodox faith was that taught in the Bible, the first four Ecumenical Councils (Nicaea to Chalcedon), and the acts of Parliament. What came to be known as the 'Elizabethan Settlement' was completed, with the adoption of a new edition of the Book of Common Prayer (1559), and the official confession of faith, the Thirty-Nine Articles, approved in 1563 to replace the Forty-Two Articles drawn up by Archbishop Cranmer.

It seems to be characteristic of English-speaking Christians that they are more interested in practical matters, like Church government and the conduct of worship, than they are in technical theological questions. While continental European theologians argued about the relation of the two natures of Christ and predestination, the English religious parties divided over matters of Church government, calling themselves *Episcopalian, Presbyterian*, and *Congregationalist*. Many people who were bitter opponents on matters of worship and Church government, held the same basic theology. So it was characteristic that the most important Anglican theological writer, Richard Hooker, was known for his big book *Laws of Ecclesiastical Polity*, an argument for Church government by bishops.

Hooker expresses the characteristic Anglican idea that the source of Christian truth is not one but many:

Wisdom has variously given her treasures to the world. . . . She shows some things through the Sacred Books of the Scriptures, some things by the glorious works of nature, she inspires them from above in some things by spiritual influence, in some things she trains and leads them only by worldly experience and practice.

We believe the truth of the Bible because the Church and Christian people have affirmed it to us:

> The Scripture does not teach us the things that are of God unless we believed men who have taught us that the words of Scriputre do signify these things.

Anglicanism is the theological 'middle way' between the theological extremes of Catholicism and Zwinglianism:

> There are therefore two opinions concerning the sufficiency of Holy Scripture, each extremely opposite to the other, and both repugnant to the truth. The schools of Rome teach that Scripture is insufficient, as if, unless Tradition were added, it did not contain all revealed and supernatural truth. . . . Others . . . likewise go to dangerous extremes, as if . . . to do anything according to any other law were not only unnecessary, but even opposite to salvation, unlawful and sinful.

Hooker maintained that no form of Church government can claim an absolutely sure basis in the Bible or the Early Church, but insisted on the necessity of a standard and official form of worship:

> By us it must be acknowledged as a work of God's singular care and providence, that the Church has always held a prescribed form of Common Prayer, although not in all things everywhere the same, yet for the most part retaining the same analogy.

THE PURITAN MOVEMENT

As we have seen, the Tudor monarchs kept Church affairs firmly in their own hands. For this reason, the Radical Reformation in England had to wait for its chance until the next century. There was always, however, an opposition to official Church policies, not only from Roman Catholics, but also from the 'left wing', who in England were called the 'Puritans'. Puritans were those who wanted to *purify* the Church of England, that is to make it more like the Reformed Churches of continental Europe, or of Scotland.

These radicals were driven out of England during the reign of Mary Tudor, and, in exile on the continent of Europe, they meditated their plans for Church reform. While there, they were much influenced by the hospitality and thinking of John Calvin and Martin Bucer (see chapter 2). Like the English Church as a whole, they concentrated on questions of worship and Church government, and soon divided into two groups:

1. The *moderates* wanted to insure that the Book of Common Prayer gave a Reformed interpretation to worship, and that there should be

reasonable guarantees of freedom of expression within an official Church governed by bishops.

2. The *radicals*, as we shall see, were not all of one opinion. But as a whole they wanted a radical 'restitution' of the Church. They wanted a simpler and more Biblical form of worship than the prayer book allowed for, greater participation by laymen, and greater independence for local congregations.

The Puritans returned to England during the reign of Elizabeth, and engaged in bitter debates with Anglican 'High Churchmen' as those with more Catholic views were called, including the Primate, John Whitgift. The Puritans' chance came when Elizabeth died without having married. The throne passed to a Scottish cousin who became James I of England, the first of the House of Stuart. The Stuart kings were strangers, and accustomed to a more humble role for the king in unruly and feudal Scotland. James himself was the son of Mary of Scotland, who was deposed by the Scots, and imprisoned and beheaded by Elizabeth. He spent his youth as a kind of hostage, passed back and forth among the Scottish nobles.

The Puritans hoped that James Stuart, from Presbyterian Scotland, would be sympathetic to their cause. In fact, however, James was heartily tired of Scottish conditions and the very powerful Church of Scotland, and he tried to rule as the Tudors had done. The Hampton Court Conference, between James and the Puritan leadership in 1604 produced only one result, but an important one: a new version of the Bible, translated by a company of scholars and published in 1611 as the 'King James', or 'Authorized' Version.

Until recently, this version continued to have the overwhelming authority in English-speaking Christendom that Luther's Bible has in Germany.

The struggle between the Puritans and the Stuarts reached its climax during the reign of James's son, Charles I. Charles was a typical 'royal victim', like Louis XVI of France and Nicholas II of Russia, both of whom also were executed by their people. Charles was a devout Anglican and a good man, but he was not very wise nor very stable. Charles's strong support for Archbishop Laud's policy of enforcing liturgical uniformity and repressing Calvinism aroused the people's hostility against both monarchy and Church. He tried to control Parliament, and instead brought on the English Civil War in 1642. Charles was defeated, and Laud was executed in 1645, but the king refused to come to terms with the Parliamentary forces. He himself was executed in 1649, and later England was transformed into a 'Commonwealth'.

During the period of the Commonwealth England had no king, but a very strong 'Lord Protector', Oliver Cromwell, who had led the cavalry in the Parliamentary forces. Under the Commonwealth, England had a greater degree of religious liberty than any other nation in Europe. The Radical Reformers saw their chance, and took it. The Commonwealth was a time of grand debate over the reform of the English Church. The English Protestants were divided into four major, and some minor, groupings:

1. *Moderate Anglicans*, who wanted to make sure that the existing Church of England would remain Calvinist in theology, and would maintain a proper balance between Scripture and Tradition in its worship.

2. *Presbyterians*, who wanted an official Church, governed, as in Scotland, not by bishops, but by elected boards of ministers and elders, called 'presbyteries' (from the Greek word *presbuteros*, meaning elder). In the first period of the Civil War the majority in Parliament were Presbyterians.

3. *Independents*, who believed that the Church should be independent from the government, and that each local congregation should be free to govern itself in matters of worship. Oliver Cromwell was an Independent.

4. *Separatists*, who felt that the existing Church of England was not a true Church, but, as some of them liked to put it, 'a synagogue of Satan'. Their positive beliefs were similar to those of the Independents, but they were less tolerant, and would not recognize other forms of the Church as legitimate. The Separatists were also known as 'Browne-ites' from their leader Robert Browne, author of *Reformation without tarrying for any*. Because of their similar views on Church government, both the last two groups came to be called 'Congregationalists'.

In addition to these major groupings there were, within Cromwell's army, other smaller bodies such as the Levellers, Diggers, and Fifth Monarchy Men. The last named agreed with Thomas Müntzer's interpretation of the second chapter of the Book of Daniel (see p. 36). More permanent groups also appeared, such as the Quakers and the Baptists, whom we shall study in chapter seven.

THE ENGLISH PRAYER BOOK

As a Reformer, King Henry VIII of England was a conservative (see p. 55). He wanted to remove the control of the Pope over the Church in England, but otherwise, in most ways he wanted to keep the doctrine, organization, and worship of the Church as it had been in the past. He strongly opposed most of the Protestant Reforms which were taking place on the Continent. During his lifetime, people in England who wanted their Church to follow the path of the Reformers on the Continent had little success. In matters of worship, the English

4.3 Thomas Cranmer, Archbishop of Canterbury, 'chief author of the English liturgy' (p. 55).

4.4 An illustration from Foxe's *Book of Martyrs* shows Cranmer's death by burning as a heretic after the Catholic Queen Mary came to the throne.

Lord receine my Spirit

Erret iohn.

Church continued to use the medieval liturgy with only a few small changes.

Only after the death of Henry VIII did greater reforms become possible. Under Edward VI, the two heads of the Council of Nobles were in favour of greater reforms.

The Archbishop of Canterbury, Thomas Cranmer, also wanted changes. Even during the time of Henry VIII, Cranmer had been quietly studying the liturgical traditions of the Church, in order to be prepared for reforms if the opportunity should come. Thus when the rulers of England became more Protestant in outlook, Cranmer was ready to act. He took the numerous liturgical books used during the Middle Ages, and, with the help of a Council, he edited them into a single volume and translated it into English.

This Book of Common Prayer, as it was called, was published in 1549. Generally, it was a conservative translation of the medieval liturgies. But in at least four ways it represented an important break with tradition:

1. For the first time in many centuries, all the services were in the language of the people.

2. The complicated system of service books, which in the past only an expert could handle, had been simplified into a book that any educated Church member could use.

3. To some extent, services had been edited under the influence of Reformation thought.

4. For the first time, the English Church had a liturgy that was the same for the entire nation.

This last change was the most unusual contribution of the Book of Common Prayer. In medieval times, services in Latin were similar throughout Europe, but local differences did exist. In those nations which were influenced by the Reformation, a number of different forms of worship came into being under the influence of different regional traditions and different reforming principles. But in England an important reason for producing the Prayer Book was to provide a similar way of worship for all English people. Thus their unity as a nation would be symbolized by their unity in worship.

The 1549 Prayer Book was not in use for long. Too many people who had been influenced by the Reformation were crying for greater changes. Cranmer himself· was sympathetic to these demands. A number of Protestant scholars from the Continent, including Martin Bucer, were in England at that time, and Cranmer responded to their evaluations of the first Prayer Book. To help preserve the unity of the Church and the nation, and to further the principles of reform, he directed the publication of a second Prayer Book in 1552. This Book was much more strongly influenced by both the thought and the practice of the Protestant Churches on the Continent of Europe (see pp. 46, 47).

Thus it can be said that the Prayer Book form of worship was the most conservative of those emerging from the Reformation. And it has also been the most enduring. Although the Prayer Book has been revised several times since 1552, the 1662 revision, imposed by a new Act of Uniformity, has been used in England till the present day. Until very recent years there have been few major changes, and even now the Prayer Book, with some local variations, provides the standard for worship for Anglican Churches throughout the world.

REFORMATION IN SCOTLAND

The first martyr to the Reformed faith in Scotland, Patrick Hamilton, died as early as 1528, but the real chance for the Reformation came with the succession of Mary Queen of Scots to the throne. She was the daughter of James V of Scotland, and the widow of the King of France. The Reformed, led by John Knox, who had studied with Calvin in Geneva and been imprisoned for a time in the galleys for his faith, took very seriously their duty to 'advise' the Queen—and they advised her off her throne. The Church of Scotland was officially established in 1560. It was a very curious established Church, since it had complete autonomy over its internal affairs.

The Church of Scotland also differed from the other Reformed Churches in its decentralized form of government. By the National Covenant of 1648 the Scots declared for 'presbyterianism'. This meant that most power was in the hands of local presbyteries, groups of 'elders' who governed the Churches in each particular district, and examined, ordained, and removed ministers. The presbyteries also held the Church property within their district. Eventually the Church of Scotland adopted the Westminster Confession of Faith, originally written for the Reformed Church of England by an assembly appointed by Parliament, but never adopted. The Reformed Churches in the English-speaking world are almost all modelled on the Church of Scotland in organization, and have adopted the Westminster Confession. The Church of Scotland suffered a number of divisions during its history, but today about 95 per cent of all Protestants in Scotland are members of that Church.

STUDY SUGGESTIONS

WORD STUDY

1. What does the term 'annulment' mean?
2. What is a 'Primate' (in the Church, not in the forest or the zoo!)?

3. Where does the term 'utopia' come from, and how did it come to be used?
4. 'Anglican' refers to members of what Church?
5. From what language does the word 'presbytery' come, and what is its importance in Church history?

REVIEW OF CONTENT

6. In what ways was the history of England different from that of continental Europe?
7. What event led to the declaration that the English king was 'single and supreme lord' of the Church of England?
8. What was the purpose of the Six Articles?
9. In what way did the Second Book of Common Prayer show Zwinglian tendencies?
10. What is meant by the 'Elizabethan Settlement'?
11. What characteristics of Anglican thought are shown by the passages in this chapter taken from Richard Hooker?
12. What was the aim of the Puritans?
13. How did England change from a monarchy to a Commonwealth?
14. What were the four main religious groupings during the Commonwealth?
15. Who was the leader of the Reformation in Scotland?
16. In what way does the Church of Scotland differ from other European Reformed Churches?
17. What were the new features of the Book of Common Prayer?

DISCUSSION AND RESEARCH

18. Is it important that all citizens of one country have the same religion? Give reasons for your answer. Would it be right for someone to change his religion at the command of the government or his family?
19. Do you believe that the Bible has in it rules for Church government? If so, give examples. Do you think all Churches should have the same form of Church government? Is your Church more episcopal, presbyterian, or congregational? What others sorts of Church government are there, in Churches in your country?
20. How does a Church decide what kind of worship it should have? Should the Sunday service always be the same in form, or should there be variety? In what ways, if any does the service in your Church resemble one of those described in this chapter?
21. If members of your Church come from other religions, or if there are important non-Christian religions in your country or region, should the Sunday service include some elements which would be familiar to non-Christians? Give reasons for your answer.

CHAPTER 5

Catholic Reformation

In the first part of this volume we are considering the Reformation of the Church. But when we think of Reformation, we must remember it was the Reformation *of* the Catholic Church. At first none of the Reformers intended to *leave* the Catholic Church; what they wanted to do was to *change* it. It is important to keep in mind that, while the Reformers were at work, the great majority of all Christians were busy living and believing as faithful Roman Catholics.

Of course this Catholic majority were affected by the Reformation. The more learned Catholics read and thought about the teachings of the Reformers, but all Catholics were affected by the fact that Christian Western Europe now contained more than one Christian Church. Catholics reacted to this division of the Church, and historians call their reactions the 'Counter-Reformation', because they went against, or 'counter to', the Reformation. However, we have called the present chapter 'Catholic Reformation' instead. This title is intended to make it clear that the concern about changing and renewing the Church was not just a concern of the Protestant Reformers.

Even while concerned to check the spread of Protestantism, Pope Hadrian VI spent his short pontificate (1522) in trying to reform the Roman Curia and correct abuses within the Church. A native of the Netherlands, Hadrian was the last non-Italian Pope.

Most of those who wanted change in the Church remained good Catholics all their lives, and the Catholic Church would probably have been very different in 1600 from what it was in 1500, even if the Protestant Reformation had never occurred. Some Catholic historians, indeed, have said that there would have been a much better Catholic Reformation if men like Luther had been able to stay within the Roman Catholic Church. But questions like that, questions beginning with 'if', are difficult to discuss in history books.

What is clear is that at least since the Great Schism of 1378 (see Vol. 2, p. 165) many Christians felt an urgent need to reform the Church. Many people were working hard to bring change to the Catholic Church at the time when the Reformers were leaving it. We will look briefly at only three ways in which Catholics reformed their Church:

1. Through new orders of monks,
2. Through the Inquisition and Index, and
3. Through a General Council of the Church.

NEW MONASTIC ORDERS

The first, and perhaps the most lasting and important, of the new developments in the Catholic Reformation was the formation of new orders of monks, some of whom were called 'regular clerks'. Neither the word 'regular' nor the word 'clerk' is used in its modern sense. 'Regular' means those who follow a *regula* (Latin for 'rule'), e.g. a monastic rule. 'Clerk' is an older English form of 'cleric' meaning a clergyman or priest. Today the word 'clerk' means someone who does writing work, usually in an office. In the Middle Ages most of those who could write had been trained in a monastery school, and so were related to the Church in a special way.

'Regular clerks' were parish priests who lived by a common discipline which included their regular parish responsibilities. They lived together, but spent their time in performing the usual priestly tasks of saying mass, hearing confessions, and preaching. They did not wear any special monastic dress, only ordinary priest's clothing. But they were usually not attached to a particular parish, and were free to move around under the direction of their superior. A number of orders of Regular Clerks were founded in the first half of the sixteenth century, because people felt that the life of the local Church was where reformation should start.

Another rather different sort of order was the Society of Jesus, now the largest Order in the Roman Catholic Church, commonly known as the 'Jesuits'.

THE JESUITS

There was no one in the Catholic Reformation whom we can compare to Luther. No one man dominated this movement. But by far the most important individual in that Reformation, whose contribution was most permanent, was a Spanish soldier, Don Inigo de Loyola (1491–1556). Loyola was a minor Spanish nobleman, whose life was much like others of his class until he was wounded so severely in battle that he became permanently lame. This happened in 1521, when he was thirty years old. He spent his long and painful convalescence in reading, and during this time read a life of Jesus and a book of the lives of the saints. This reading led to his conversion, not in the sense of a change in religious beliefs, as with Luther and Calvin, but in the sense of a commitment to the full-time practice of the religious life. As a sign of this conversion he changed his name from the Spanish Inigo to the Greek Ignatius, in honour of the great bishop of Antioch, whose main concern was for the unity and purity of the Church (see Vol. 1, p. 64).

To prepare himself for his new work, Ignatius studied at four

'The most important individual in the Catholic Reformation was Ignatius de Loyola' (p. 68).

5.1 Contrast the sober portrait marking his appointment as founder and head of the Jesuits with (below):

5.2 Baciccio's later painting of the saint in glory—typical of the 'baroque' style of church decoration which became fashionable in the seventeenth and eighteenth centuries.

universities, practised the spiritual life, and talked to others about the life of obedience to Jesus and service to the Church. As a result he gathered about him a group of nine other remarkable young men, who formed the core of the new Society. He also prepared a spiritual manual for their use, the *Spiritual Exercises*. Ignatius wrote that Spiritual Exercises are:

Any method of preparing and disposing the soul to free itself from all inordinate affections, and . . . to seek and to find the will of God concerning the ordering of life for the salvation of one's soul.

The sub-title of the *Spiritual Exercises* puts this more briefly: 'To conquer oneself and regulate one's life.'

The exercises of Ignatius are distinctive because he always directs that contemplation should be undertaken for the sake of activity. The Jesuits were, and perhaps still are, among the most active Christians around. The method of the *Exercises* also is distinctive. It demands that in contemplation people must make full use of their imagination, so that what is contemplated is reproduced by all five senses: sight, hearing, taste, touch, and smell. Each exercise is accompanied by a 'colloquy', or conversation, conducted between the believer and God, Christ, or the Virgin Mary. The exercises are designed to occupy thirty days, and every Jesuit is required to make a retreat and go through the exercises every year, although not for a full thirty days each time. The subject of the first week's exercises is sin, and the sins of the angels, of Adam, of mankind, and of oneself are contemplated. The first week ends with the contemplation of hell. The subject of the second week is Christ; of the third week Christ's death; and of the fourth week His resurrection.

Ignatius thought of his Society first as a missionary Order which would have some of the spirit of the military orders during the Crusades (see Vol. 2, p. 83). The first companions vowed to go to the Holy Land to convert the Muslims. But it proved impossible for them to make the trip, so the Society instead pursued its second aim; to be completely obedient to the Pope. The Society was officially recognized in 1540. At that time, what the Pope was primarily interested in was not the conversion of Asia, but the spiritual and disciplinary renewal of the Church, and the reconversion of Protestants. Jesuits became the most noted and efficient school teachers of Europe, and they took a leading part in the reconversion of Austria, Bohemia, Hungary, Southern Germany, and Poland. They were unsuccessful in England, where they engaged in much political plotting, and where many of them were put to death for their faith and activities.

The Jesuits were especially important among the Roman Catholic Orders because of their very high level of professional training, their systematic practice of a method of contemplation, their political activities, and their radical obedience to the Church. The last section of the *Spiritual Exercises* is entitled 'Rules for Thinking with the Church'. It contains a sentence which has since become famous: 'We ought always to hold what seems to us white to be black, if the Hierarchical Church so defines it.'

The Society never forgot its commitment to foreign missions. Jesuits became the most famous of all missionaries to India and China, and were prominent also in South and North America (see chapters 6 and 10).

REFORMS IN ADMINISTRATION

Beginning with Pope Paul III, who ruled the Church from 1534 to 1549, the Roman Church was led by a series of energetic, intelligent, and able reformers. The papacy never again sank to the low level it had reached at the beginning of the fifteenth century. Instead, the papacy became the model which national governments imitated. The first ambassadors in the modern sense of permanent representatives to a foreign government were the papal *nuncios*. Fifteen *congregations* were created to administer Church affairs. The morals of the Pope and those at the papal court became the model for the whole Church, and no longer were a source of embarrassment.

One thing, however, did continue to hinder the reform of the Catholic Church. This was the fact that the Popes were not only the spiritual and administrative heads of the Church; at the same time they were the political heads of the Papal States in Central Italy. For three hundred more years they were to be deeply involved in local Italian politics.

Apart from particular moral and disciplinary reforms, the most important change which the reforming Popes made was when they set up the 'Holy Office' of the Roman Inquisition. 'Inquisition' means inquiry or investigation. Since the thirteenth century, when heresy was strong in Southern France, all bishops had been required to maintain a regular Inquisition, or court, which inquired into the faith of Church members. The inquisition was directed toward Christians, not non-Christians, and inquired into their faith and practices. It did not itself impose punishment, although it might use torture in its investigations, as all government legal systems of the time did. The aim of the inquisition was to bring heretics to repentance. Sometimes defiant heretics were handed over to governments for punishment. The Spanish rulers in their 'reconquest' of Spain from the Muslims, used the Inquisition on a national scale, and under the control of the king.

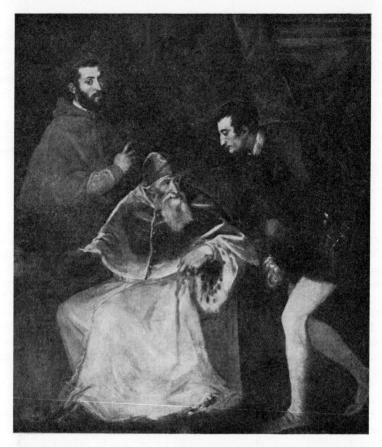

5.3 'In 1542 Pope Paul III formally organized the Roman Inquisition to eliminate moral offences, simony, and heresy' (p. 73).
Titian's portrait of Paul III includes the Pope's two grandsons, who both became cardinals.

In 1542 Pope Paul III formally organized the Roman or 'Papal' Inquisition. For the first time, the whole Church was subject to one papal court. The Holy Office was instructed to eliminate moral offences, simony (the selling of Church offices), and heresy among both clergy and lay-people. The Holy Office consisted of six cardinals and a staff of Dominican friars. Under its first head, Cardinal Caraffa, (who became Pope Paul IV), the Holy Office spared no one. Rank made no difference. Only the Pope could alter any judgement or sentence passed by the Inquisition. Even the Primate of Spain was condemned. And the nobility and higher clergy of Italy were terrified of its investigations. In Italy Protestantism was quickly stamped out.

A second development which helped to ensure the unity of the Church was the Index (from *Index librorum prohitorum*, a 'list of forbidden books'). Catholics were forbidden to read books written by heretics, books which were anonymous, and those specifically condemned by the Church. The first Index was made up by Caraffa as Pope Paul IV in 1559. Later, a permanent Congregation of the Index was established, to keep a regular watch on the books being published.

The Index was finally abolished by Pope Paul VI in 1966. There is still a Holy Office, though now under another name, but it works quite differently from that of the sixteenth century. The Roman Inquisition, the Index, and the decrees of the Council of Trent (see the next section) for the first time gave the Roman Catholic Church instruments with which to enforce uniformity in its faith and life.

THE COUNCIL OF TRENT

During the Reformation almost everyone wanted, or said they wanted, a General Council of the Church. But by 'Council' they did not all mean the same thing, nor did they all want it for the same reason. The Protestants wanted an opportunity for free theological discussion. The Emperor Charles V wanted to reform the moral standards of the priests. He hoped this might persuade the Protestants to return to the Roman Church and reunite his empire.

The Popes had come very much to dislike the word 'Council', because the later Councils had claimed supreme authority over the Church. The reforming Popes, however, concluded that there was no other way to solve the problems of the Church. Calling the Council, however, proved difficult. France and the Empire were at war most of the time. Finally, during a truce, the Council was proclaimed, and was held on neutral ground, in the city of Trento, in the Italian Alps.

The council of Trent was regarded by the Roman Catholic Church as the nineteenth Ecumenical Council. When it opened in December, 1545, there were only thirty-one official delegates, but 255 delegates signed the final decree eighteen years later. The Council had a stormy history for both political and theological reasons. One session was adjourned because war broke out, and another because of plague. Between the second and third sessions, the Emperor Charles V abdicated his throne. From that time onwards, Spanish Hapsburgs were kings of Spain and Austrian Hapsburgs ruled the Empire. Western Europe was never under one government again.

The Council itself was made up of groups with entirely different aims. The Emperor and other rulers wanted moral reform and the readmission of the Protestants. The Pope wanted a strongly unified Church to defy the Protestants. The rulers could exert political pressure on the Council, but Trent was near enough for many Italian bishops to 'commute' to the Council to vote on the Pope's side on important issues. The Council was actually in session for parts of six years.

THE DECREES OF TRENT

The decisions or decrees of the Council of Trent were all directed against the special teachings of the Reformers. The most important ones dealt with the crucial questions of the Bible, original sin, justification by faith, and the sacraments. In all cases traditional Catholic teaching was reaffirmed, but it was now defined in a new, precise, and strict way. Only the Decree on Justification shows that the Council studied the Reformers' teaching seriously. The individual sacraments were discussed in detail, and such teachings as the existence of purgatory, prayers to the saints, and the validity of indulgences, which the Reformers rejected, were all upheld.

THE BIBLE

The Council's decisions on the Bible were perhaps the most striking, and had the most permanent influence. The Council declared that:

1. The official version of the Bible to be used by Catholics was Jerome's fourth century Latin translation, called the Vulgate.

2. The Bible included the Apocrypha, that is, books and parts of books which were included in the Greek translation of Old Testament, called the Septuagint, but were not in the Hebrew text.

3. The Bible must always be interpreted according to the teaching of the Church:

> No one, relying on his own skill ... shall presume to interpret the Sacred Scriptures differently from the way in which Holy Mother Church does and has done ... even though such interpretations were never to be at any time published.

JUSTIFICATION

The Fathers at Trent clearly had Luther very much in mind as they defined the Catholic view of justification. Beginning with Augustine, as the Reformers had done, the Council rejected Luther's specific teachings. In opposition to Augustine, Luther, and Calvin, the Council taught that the saving grace of God could be rejected, and also that grace could be increased by good works, lost through sin, and restored through the sacrament of Penance:

> If anyone says that the sinner is justified through faith alone, meaning that nothing else is required in order to obtain the grace of justification . . . or even that the grace by which we are justified is only the favour of God, let him be anathema (that is, condemned or cursed).

According to this teaching, faith is not simply confidence in God's mercy, and Christ is not only the One who forgives our sins. Christ is also the new lawgiver. For the sinner, God's forgiveness does not remove the necessity of paying back for our sins, either here or in purgatory.

THE SACRAMENTS

The Council declared that all seven sacraments were instituted by Christ himself. It reaffirmed the doctrine of transubstantiation (see pp. 25, 26), and stated that the Lord's Supper must be understood as a sacrifice:

> The victim is one and the same, the same now offering through the ministry of priests, who then offered himself on the cross, only the manner of offering is different.

THE ROMAN CHURCH IN 1600

The great period of Catholic Reformation came after, rather than before, the Council of Trent. The decisions of the Council and its disciplinary actions were very effective. The standards of priestly and monastic life were raised, as well as the level of theological education. The limits of the faith were clearly defined. Catholics were truly one, with a sense of direction, and great determination and energy. One fruit of Catholic Reformation was a new and intense form of mysticism, which first arose in Spain under the influence of a Carmelite nun, Teresa of Avila, and her disciple John of the Cross, who taught new forms of interior prayer. The trend was also expressed in the new and intensely passionate art forms of the Baroque school in painting, sculpture, and architecture.

The first concern of the Church, of course, was to restore unity of faith to Western Europe. This attempt was not successful; we have already studied the new religious frontiers in Europe (see pp. 31, 32).

Nevertheless, the Catholic Church made an astonishing recovery, and the parts of Europe which remained Roman Catholic in 1600 continue so today. Christian losses to Islam came to an end when the attempt of the Turkish fleet to capture Cyprus was warded off in 1571.

The continuing internal reform of the Church was very striking. A catechism was produced, expressing the faith as defined at Trent. Liturgical books were revised, including the missal (the liturgy of the mass) and the breviary (the daily prayerbook of the monks). The Latin Bible, the Vulgate, was also revised. Bishops were instructed to hold regular synods, or meetings of priests, in their dioceses. They were also instructed to visit their clergy regularly and to maintain a theological seminary in each diocese. The central administration of the Church was so streamlined that its running expenses were reduced by half.

In 1622 a very unusual event occurred. In St Peter's Church in Rome, which had been completely rebuilt during the Reformation, five saints were canonized in a single ceremony. Four of them were made saints within fifty years of their death, which was unusually soon in Roman Catholic procedure. Four were leaders of the Catholic Reformation: Ignatius Loyola, Teresa of Avila, Francis Xavier, the great Jesuit missionary and companion of Ignatius (see p. 70), and Philip Neri, a reformer in Rome and founder of an order of Regular Clerks. The Church was quick to recognize the great changes that had taken place, and to honour those who had helped to bring them about.

The Reformation is sometimes spoken of as a 'tragedy'. People who say this mean that the divisions which resulted from the Reformers' criticisms of Rome were a major set-back for the Church. However, since Luther aimed his theological attack at the basis of the Roman Church itself, the break seems to have been inevitable. Luther denied that the Church possessed things called 'merits' which could be given to believers. He also rejected the idea that the Church was permanently divided into two classes, the ordained clergy and the ordinary members of the Church. Perhaps for the fullness of the Church's life it was necessary to divide, at least for a time, in order to work out a new understanding of these ideas of faith, justification, and sanctification (see pp. 7, 18), and to discover their meaning for the life of believers.

What certainly was tragic, however, was the new rigidness and defensiveness of the Catholic Church. The teachings of the Council of Trent and the new agencies of the Church were all negative. They were not only directed against the attacks of the Reformers and the new Protestant Churches. They also condemned the work of scientists like Copernicus and Galileo, whose new discoveries and theories about the nature of the universe seemed to conflict with a literal interpretation of the Bible. The positive values of the new mysticism, zeal, and forms of artistic expression grew up on unpromising soil. The Church took this

5.4 'The Council of Trent was actually in session for parts of six years' (p. 74).
It was held on 'neutral' ground in the Church of Santa Maria Maggiore at Trento in the Italian Alps.

same defensive position against modern trends in thought in the nineteenth century. Christians are at their best in attack and weakest in defence.

STUDY SUGGESTIONS

WORD STUDY

1. Why is the phrase 'Catholic Reformation' instead of 'Counter-Reformation' used in this chapter?
2. What does the phrase 'Regular Clerks' mean?
3. What does the Latin word *Index* mean, and what is its significance in Church History?
4. The word *anathema* is a Hebrew word taken over in English. What does it mean?

REVIEW OF CONTENT

5. In what important ways did Catholics reform their Church?
6. Describe the meditation methods taught by Ignatius Loyola.
7. Why did the Jesuits not specialize in foreign missions as they had at first intended?
8. What was the Roman Inquisition?
9. Why was it so difficult to call a General Council of the Church?
10. How did the teaching of the Council of Trent on Justification differ from Luther's teaching on this subject?
11. According to the Council of Trent, what happens in the Lord's Supper?
12. In what ways did the Catholic Reformation make the Church 'modern'?

DISCUSSION AND RESEARCH

13. How did the Catholic understanding of the Bible, as defined at Trent, differ from Protestant views? Why do you think it was important to make the Vulgate the official Bible of the Catholic Church?
14. Jesus said: 'You shall know them by their fruits.' Paul said: 'We are justified by faith, without the works of the law.' James said: 'Faith without works is dead.' From these and other New Testament passages on these subjects, explain your own idea of what the New Testament teaches about the relation of faith and works. (Use a Concordance)
15. According to Luther, Christians are saved by faith, which produces good works but is not dependent on them. The Council of Trent ruled that faith and works together are necessary for salvation. Is there a real difference between these views? If so, how important is that difference?

16. The Council of Trent ruled that it was right to 'compel' people who had been baptized to become confirmed members of the Church. If you believe that right faith and membership in the Church is necessary for salvation, what would be your attitude towards someone who believed wrongly, or who wanted to leave the Church?

17. A student, reading about the 'Inquisition', compared the Church's efforts to force people to hold certain religious beliefs, to the efforts of communist governments to force people to hold certain political views. What is your opinion?

CHAPTER 6

Mission or Empire?

PORTUGAL LOOKS EAST

In the second volume of this Guide, we studied the lives of four European navigators, two in the service of Spain and two from Portugal (see Vol. 2, pp. 180–186). Both countries had the same aims. Portugal and Spain were both looking for a new way to Asia, both were interested in trade, and both desired to carry the Gospel through all the world. These two peoples both thought of their explorations as crusades: crusades against Islam. They had both just finished the 'reconquest' of their own lands by driving out the Arab invaders who had crossed from North Africa and dominated most of the Iberian peninsula for centuries. This campaign had been conducted in the name of the Christian faith. We know that the period of the Crusades had been over since 1291, and that they had failed in their aim. But political and military contact with Muslim powers in the Eastern Mediterranean had continued.

We should also remember that the Portuguese and Spanish were interested primarily in trade, and not in colonization. Unlike the English later, in most cases they were not seeking land in order to settle and build new homes for themselves. But just for that reason, their colonies on the whole did not last as long.

Vasco da Gama and others gradually set up a series of Portuguese trading posts and forts, stretching from the western coast of Africa to the Molucca Islands in East Indonesia. The Portuguese also had trading rights on the southern island of Japan. The most important of these centres were Angola and Mozambique in Southern Africa, Goa in India, Malacca in Malaya, and Macao on the coast of China.

The Portuguese trade with Asia was not very successful. Their trading posts were under constant attack, both by local rulers and European rivals. They found such a long chain of ports very difficult to administer, and most of the profits of the spice trade were taken by individual merchants rather than by the governments. Soon the Portuguese government was spending more on its trade than it was receiving back in profits, and the Portuguese king was deeply in debt to the Flemish bankers. But these trading posts did provide bases for the Christian mission to China and to India. Portuguese explorers prepared the way for one of the most extraordinary of all Christian missionaries, Francis Xavier (see pp. 84, 85).

THE PADROADO

As we have already seen, the desire of both Portugal and Spain to find new ways to reach Asia led to intervention by the Pope (see p. 14). In 1493 Pope Alexander VI allocated all non-Christian lands to the East of a line drawn West of the Azores Islands in the Atlantic to the patronage of Portugal, and all the lands West of this line to Spain. The aim of this arrangement was:

> to bring to the Christian faith the peoples who inhabit these islands and mainland . . . and to send to the said islands and to the mainland wise, upright, and virtuous men who will be capable of instructing the indigenous peoples in good morals and the Catholic faith.

The Portuguese and Spanish agreed to extend this line westward in such a way that most of what is now Brazil was within the Portuguese area. The line was later extended over the North Pole and through the Pacific Ocean in such a way that the Spanish West included the Philippine Islands, and the Portuguese East included the Molucca Islands.

The Papal Bulls of 1493 appointed the Portuguese and Spanish rulers as 'patrons' of the Church in their respective areas. This meant that they had to bear all the expenses of sending missionaries, and building, maintaining, and defending the Church. This also gave them full control of the Churches they had established, and even the right to decide whether or not the Popes' decrees should be put into effect in their areas.

This patronage system (commonly called the *padroado*, using the Portuguese form of the word 'patronage'), was not very different from the relationships between the Catholic Church and Catholic nations in Europe after the Council of Trent. By this time the Popes were no longer able to tell rulers what to do in their own countries, or to rule the various national Churches directly. The Popes found that countries like France and Spain got along better if the Catholic rulers had some control over the Churches in their lands.

But it is one thing to oversee the Church near by, and another to be responsible for Churches thousands of miles across the sea. By the end of the sixteenth century, the Portuguese government was no longer able to finance or supply priests for all the Churches in its colonies. But Portugal clung stubbornly to its monopoly. All missionaries to the East had to sail from Lisbon, and to have permission from the Portuguese government to do so. This meant much trouble for the mission to India and China, but the arrangement continued down to the nineteenth century.

SPAIN LOOKS WEST

One difference between the history of colonization by the Portuguese, and that of the Spaniards, was that the Portuguese succeeded in what they intended to do and the Spaniards did not. The Portuguese successfully set up a trading system which extended to Indonesia and China. The Spaniards, on the other hand, found themselves committed to a vast land-mass which they finally realized was not the outskirts of Asia, as they had thought, but two unexpected continents which were totally unknown to them. The Spaniards, and later the French and English, wasted a lot of time in trying to get around the Americas in order to find a convenient trade-route to Asia.

The great Portuguese adventurers at this time were sailors. Even Magellan, who sailed on behalf of Spain, was himself a Portuguese. Columbus was an Italian.

The great Spanish adventurers, on the other hand, were soldiers. These soldiers, who came to be called *conquistadores* (Spanish for 'conquerors'), quickly subdued the islands of the Caribbean Sea, Central America, and the Pacific coast of South America. They then began to move into what is today the south-western part of the United States.

The success of these conquistadors, like Hernando Cortez in Mexico and Francisco Pizarro in Peru, was especially striking, because they led tiny bands of men against the huge Aztec and Inca empires. These empires had, in some ways, a higher civilization than Spain itself. The chief advantages of the Spaniards were their determination and crusading zeal, and their superior technology. Neither the Aztecs nor the Incas had yet discovered the wheel, and the only animals in the Americas trained to carry loads were llamas used by the Incas. With gunpowder and horses, and a hunger for glory and gold, the Spaniards conquered Latin America.

The conquistadors were a very unusual group of men, in addition to being very brave and resourceful. Today we may find it surprising that they were equally eager to spread the Gospel, to conquer new lands for their king, and to gain riches for themselves. But they had no difficulty in combining these very dissimilar motives. One of the companions of Cortez, Bernal Diaz, survived to write an important book, a first-hand account of the conquest of Mexico, called *The True History of the Conquest of New Spain*. In it, he asks himself reflectively:

Where are now my companions? They have fallen in battle, or been devoured by the cannibal, or been thrown to fatten the wild beasts in their cages! They whose remains should rather have been gathered

'The Spanish adventurers were soldiers . . . like Francisco Pizarro in Peru, they were equally eager to spread the Gospel, conquer new lands, and gain riches' (p. 82). 'They were also very cruel' (p. 84).

6.1 Pizarro's looks were certainly soldierly . . . .

6.2 . . . and illustrations of the period show the Spaniards under his command maltreating the Peruvians they had conquered.

under monuments emblazoned with their achievements, which deserve to be commemorated in letters of gold; for they died in the service of God and of his Majesty the King of Spain, and to give light to those who sat in darkness, and also to acquire that wealth which most men covet.

Cortez was so devout that he wept at the sight of a cross beside the road, and, like some other explorers, himself preached the Gospel to the native people when no priest or friar was around. He was also cruel, and made very clear what he hoped personally to gain by his expedition. The great crusading bishop de las Casas (see p. 86), in his *History of the Indies*, reports that Cortez asked the representative of the Aztec king Montezuma for gold dust, explaining, 'the Spaniards were troubled with a disease of the heart, for which gold is the specific remedy'.

FRANCIS XAVIER, SJ (1506–1552)

As we have seen, the Portuguese opened the way for one of the most remarkable missionary expeditions in Christian history. Francis Xavier, like his leader Ignatius, was one of the daring and restless Basque people from the mountainous north of Spain, who cause trouble to the Spanish government to this day. He met Ignatius when they were both students at the University of Paris, and was converted by him to the 'regular' life. They were ordained together in Venice in 1537. Of the original ten companions (see p. 70) Francis Xavier was the only one who worked in the foreign missionary enterprise which had been the original intention of them all.

In 1541, Ignatius, as Minister General of the Society of Jesus, sent Francis Xavier to respond to the king of Portugal's invitation to evangelize the Indies. Francis arrived in Goa in May 1542, and immediately began work among fishermen on the coast. It is said that in thirty days he converted more Hindus than his Portuguese colleagues had done in thirty years, although he knew little of the Tamil language.

Francis Xavier was the model of all mass evangelists. He had the Lord's Prayer, the Apostles' Creed, and the Ave Maria translated into the local language. He then taught them to children, who in turn instructed their parents. When a whole family could recite the three basic Catholic statements, they were baptized. The Jesuits claimed that in his ten years of missionary service, Francis Xavier baptized 700,000 people.

After working in South India and Ceylon, Francis Xavier went on to Malacca, and to the Indonesian Molucca Islands. A Japanese whom he met in Malacca attracted his attention to Japan, and he studied the language and sailed there in 1549. Francis Xavier's experience in Japan changed his attitude towards evangelism to one which became the distinctive mark of the great Jesuit missionaries from then on. He wrote:

> Firstly, the people whom we met so far are the best who have yet been discovered, and it seems to me that we shall never find among heathens another race equal to the Japanese. . . . They are a people of very good will, very sociable, and very desirous of knowledge; they are very fond of hearing about the things of God, chiefly when they understand them. . . . Granted that there are sins and vices among them, when one reasons with them, pointing out that what they do is evil, they are convinced by this reasoning.

Later Jesuits were to take the same attitude towards the higher classes in China and in India. Perhaps Francis Xavier understood and respected the Japanese so well because Japan was the one country whose language he had studied before he began work there.

In 1552, Francis Xavier was recalled to Goa to take up administrative duties as Superior of the Jesuits in the East, but in the same year he left on his final missionary journey. He travelled to Malacca, and then took ship to China. He had heard that China was the source of all of the culture of the East, and he wanted to carry the Gospel there as well. But when within sight of the coast of China, he fell ill, and was buried on St John's Island, south of Macao. The Church which he had planted persisted in each place he visited, except in the Indonesian islands, where parts were wiped out by local Muslim rulers, and the rest was made Protestant by the later Dutch rulers. In Japan, the Church which he planted in 1549 was suppressed with severe persecutions which began in 1614. But the story of Christianity in Japan will be told in Chapter 10.

SPANISH MISSIONS IN AMERICA

The detailed history of Spanish missions in the Americas is a long one. Here we shall consider only some of the more striking episodes, the work of the Franciscans and Dominicans in Mexico, and of the Jesuits in Uruguay and Paraguay.

As we have seen, the preaching of the Gospel was a chief motive in the Spaniards' conquest of the Americas. Columbus took friars with him on his second expedition; and on the third, he built a church. The Church in the West Indies had its own bishop in 1510, when the chief chaplain of the Spanish army became Patriarch there.

Cortez took friars with him on his conquest of Mexico in 1519, and the first resident priests arrived in Mexico at Cortez's request in 1524. The bishopric of Mexico City became an archbishopric in 1548, and for some time the Church in the Philippines was under its jurisdiction.

The rapid and total collapse of the haughty Aztec Empire led to the discrediting of Aztec culture. Mexico was ripe for evangelization. In 1529 Franciscan friars were reporting 8,000 to 14,000 baptisms a day in some areas. Mexico was also fortunate in its Church leadership. The first bishop of Mexico City, Zumarraga, was a follower of Erasmus, who encouraged the translation of the Bible into the languages of Mexico, and the training of clergy among the local Amerindian people. (The inhabitants of the Americas were known as 'Indians' by the first Spanish adventurers, because they thought they had reached the East Indies. The name persisted, but recently the compound of 'American' and 'Indian' in the form 'Amerindian' has been introduced, to distinguish them from the real Indians.) Even better known was the priest, and later bishop, Bartolomeo de las Casas (1474–1566).

De las Casas came to the West Indies as an adventurer, but received a call to the priesthood through hearing a sermon which condemned the injustices practised by the Spaniards against the local population. He became a great champion of the Amerindians, believing that:

> No nation exists . . . which may not be persuaded and brought to a good order and way of life, and made domestic, mild and tractable, provided the method that is proper and natural to men be used; namely, love, gentleness, and kindness.

De las Casas condemned the Spaniards' system of land-holding and their use of Amerinidan labourers in something like slavery. The Spanish colonists of course strongly resisted him. But de las Casas successfully appealed to the king of Spain, and the Laws of the Indies (1542), i.e. the constitution of the Spanish empire, reflect his influence.

Many of the early missionaries showed real Christian compassion and helpfulness, but in the end its practical effect was not great. According to one recent study, the Amerindian population of Central Mexico declined from 11,000,000 in 1519 at the time of Cortez's arrival, to 2,500,000 by the end of the sixteenth century.

Very unfortunately this depopulation of Central America led to the importation of slaves from Africa. This trade had been begun by the English, and was taken up by the Portuguese and others. For whatever reasons, this trade was not generally felt to be unChristian for over two centuries. An English Calvinist in the seventeenth century wrote to another who was trying to free African slaves: 'Religion consists not so much in an outward conformity of actions as in truth in the inward parts.' It was not generally thought that Christians must necessarily *act* in what we now regard as a Christian manner.

For another glimpse of Spanish evangelism in the Americas, we will turn to an unusual experiment in eastern South America. Jesuits began working in the Americas within ten years of the founding of their

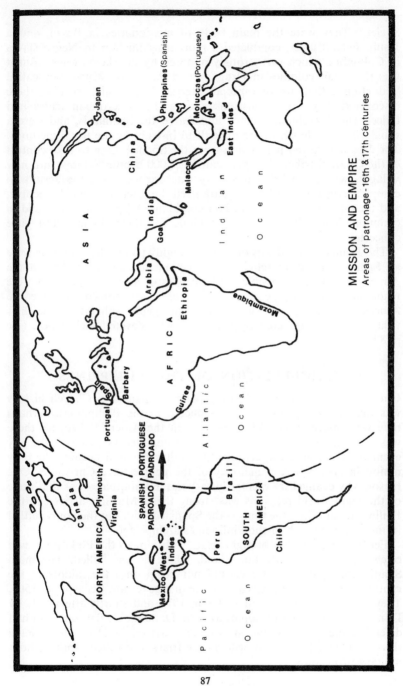

MISSION AND EMPIRE
Areas of patronage - 16th & 17th centuries

Society. They were the main body of missionaries in Brazil, and a Jesuit, Peter Claver, conducted a pioneering mission to Negro slaves in Colombia, which was strongly opposed by the slave-owners. But it was the Jesuit colonies in Uruguay and Paraguay, which they called 'reductions', that are of especial interest. The Jesuits working there discovered why earlier missions among the Amerindian tribes had failed. The Amerindians hated and feared the Spaniards, and were a wandering people who were difficult to instruct by the usual methods. The Jesuits received permission from the Spanish king to take control of the Guaraní tribe. They persuaded 120,000 people to move into new villages, where a Christian society was created, with the Jesuits in complete control. The Jesuits guaranteed the safety of the tribespeople, and taught them farming and housebuilding. All property was held in common. The villages became famous for their singing, and gave concerts.

The Jesuits' method was of course a highly paternalistic one, as were all Spanish efforts in religious instruction and social welfare in the Americas. And the possible consequences of such an approach were made plain in a tragic way. The Jesuits were forced to leave the Americas in 1768, and very quickly the gentle inhabitants of their villages were slaughtered by Spaniards who coveted their lands. (see p. 82).

EVANGELIZATION OF THE PHILIPPINES

One of the most successful evangelistic campaigns in Church history was that which Spanish friars conducted in the Philippines. Perhaps they were more successful there than in the Americas because there was no gold in the Philippines for the conquerors to covet. In any event, by the eighteenth century the Philippines had become the only nation in Asia where a majority of the people were Christians. One reason why evangelism was fairly easy in the Philippines was that none of the main world religions was strong there. Muslims arrived in the Philippines at about the time as the Spaniards did, but they only settled in the extreme south of the Philippines archipelago.

Ferdinand Magellan brought friars with him to the Philippines and celebrated mass on Mactan Island, where he was killed. The main Spanish occupation, however, did not begin until the middle of the century. Augustinians arrived with the first governor, Legaspe, in 1565. They were followed by Franciscans in 1577, and shortly afterwards by Dominicans. The first bishop of Manila, Domingo de Salazar, who had defended the Amerindians in America, arrived in 1581. He forbade slavery in the islands, and ordered the friars to do their work without military protection.

In 1586 it was reported that more than 400,000 people had been baptized. In 1591 Manila became an archdiocese. From then on, conversions continued more or less steadily, reaching a million in 1750. After that time the pace slowed down, because of resistance by the Muslims in the South and the mountain peoples of Northern Luzon Island.

FRENCH EXPLORATION AND MISSIONS

The period of European colonization 'overseas' was not, of course, only a Spanish and Portuguese affair. But these two nations did begin the movement, and they dominated the history of sixteenth century voyages. We turn now to speak briefly about the expansion of three other European nations, who began their overseas activities later, but soon became very important. The first of these was France.

France was a great European power, and a wealthy nation, but was never as deeply occupied with the sea trade as Portugal and Spain were. Furthermore, France was preoccupied with European power politics, and with her own religious civil wars, up to the end of the sixteenth century. One exception to this was the alliance between the king of France and the Sultan of Turkey. The Turks were threatening Hungary and Austria, and were engaged in piracy in the Mediterranean. Through a treaty in 1534, France became protector of the Holy Places in Palestine, and of Christians throughout the Turkish Empire. The 'Most Christian' King of France was allied to a Muslim nation against which the Pope had just proclaimed a crusade! French influence in the Near East has continued down to the present day.

The first centre of French attention in the sixteenth century was the region of North America along the St Lawrence River, in what is now Canada. Frenchmen visited this region as early as 1524, but they made no plans for regular colonization until the following century. Their first attempts in the seventeenth century, also, did not prove to be permanent. On two occasions the hostility of the English settlers further south prevented permanent settlement by the French. Temporary mission work was done by the Jesuits and the Recollects. The return of the French will be described in chapter 10.

DUTCH AND ENGLISH COLONIZATION

At the beginning of the sixteenth century, the Netherlands belonged to Spain, and until the middle of the seventeenth century, the Dutch were engaged in an eighty years war for independence. They were a commercial and seafaring people, and in 1602 founded the Netherlands United East India Company. This trading company took over much of the Portuguese trading area, and established itself in the Molucca Islands in 1605. Batavia (later called Jakarta) was founded in Java in 1619, and the Company took control over Malacca, Ceylon, and Formosa.

This was a purely commercial venture, chartered by the Dutch government, but for private profit. The Dutch were regarded as having no religious interest. In the seventeenth century the Japanese forbade all mission work, foreign residence, and contacts between Japanese and foreigners. They made, however, one exception for the Protestant Dutch. Dutch traders were permitted to land, but their first act upon landing had to be to trample on the cross!

The Netherlands United East India Company was required by its charter to provide for the religious needs of its Dutch employees at each trading post. So chaplains were sent to Asia. The first Protestant congregation in Asia was established at Ambon in the Moluccas in 1605, and the congregation in this same place is still in existence today. These Dutch chaplains were not missionaries, but, especially in the East Indies—now Indonesia—local people were attracted to their services. Services were begun in the Common Malay trading language of the Indies. Whether or not the Dutch were lacking in religious zeal, their great struggle against Spain made them strongly anti-Catholic. They tried to eliminate the Catholic Church in the regions which they controlled, and in Indonesia they were completely successful in doing so.

The British, like the Dutch, conducted exploration and colonization as individuals and groups, and mainly for commercial purposes. In this, the Dutch and British differed from the Portuguese, Spanish, and French, whose colonization was under the direct control of their kings. British colonization also differed from all others: one of its chief purposes was to establish permanent colonies where people from the already crowded British Isles might move to seek a new and challenging future.

There were British and other fishing colonies on the coast of North America in the sixteenth century, but full-scale British colonization in North America and the West Indies did not begin until the seventeenth century. Many of the charters of these companies of 'adventurers', as they were called, included a clause requiring that the Gospel should be preached to the Amerindians. However, this was not done in any organized way until the following (eighteenth) century.

Europeans continued their colonization in Asia, Africa, and Latin America right into the twentieth century. In this chapter we have dealt mainly with the sixteenth century beginnings of this movement, and shall look again at the subject in chapter 10 for Asia, while the later worldwide spread of European influence, and of the Christian Church, is left to Volume 4. But it is already clear that the Christian faith came to many regions of the world as part of a mixture which included political influence, military power, and commercial and personal ambitions, and also, of course, sin.

STUDY SUGGESTIONS

WORD STUDY

1. From what language does the word *padroado* come, and what does it mean?
2. What is the meaning of conquistadors?
3. Why is the term 'Amerindians' used in this chapter?

REVIEW OF CONTENT

4. What were the aims of the Portuguese and Spanish adventurers?
5. Did the Portuguese expeditions achieve what they set out to do? Give reasons and examples to explain your answer.
6. What were (a) the rights and (b) the duties of the rulers under the *padroado*?
7. Why was it so easy for the Spanish to overthrow the Aztec Empire?
8. What were the missionary methods of Francis Xavier?
9. What did Francis Xavier think of the Japanese people, and why?
10. What was the chief mission of Bartolomeo de las Casas?
11. Describe the Jesuit experiment with the Guaranì tribe.
12. Why was the evangelization of the Philippines so rapid?
13. What was the special relationship between France and the lands of the Near East?
14. What was the main centre of French colonization?
15. How were the first Protestant converts made in Indonesia?
16. In what ways did British colonization differ from that of most other European nations?

DISCUSSION AND RESEARCH

17. The European adventurers brought their culture and commerce as well as their faith to the rest of the world. Is it possible to preach the Gospel to someone *without* at the same time communicating your own ideas, standards, and values which come from your own cultural background?
18. What are likely to be the results of conversion by (a) political and (b) military means?
19. The Spanish missionaries were known for their 'paternalism'. Can you think of other examples of paternalism in Church and mission. Do you know any from your own area? What are the effects of paternalism?

CHAPTER 7
American Puritanism

It was in England that the two movements of colonization and reformation came together. The result was the American Protestant denominations, which were the greatest centres of Protestant influence in the nineteenth and twentieth centuries. Because English colonization was conducted by private organizations, and not by the government, it was possible for these Protestant Churches to develop in their own way, apart from the authority of the English Church and government.

Most of the English Puritans were middle class people; small and medium landowners, businessmen, and craftsmen. They were anxious for new opportunities, and were restless under the Church and state of the Catholic Stuart kings. The same group led the rebellion of Parliament against King Charles I. Behind every colonization attempt of this group was a mixture of religious and economic motives. But with the exception of the one colony of Maryland, the leaders of all these colonization movements were Puritans of one kind or another. The United States today is a mixture of immigrants from many places, and those of English background are now a small minority. But the first colonies stamped the American character with certain Puritan features, which have influenced the nation throughout the first two hundred years of its history (1776 to the present day).

THE FIRST TWO ENGLISH COLONIES

The first permanent English colonies represented the extreme points of Puritan differences. The Virginia colony was officially Anglican, while Plymouth, Massachusetts, was colonized by Separatists (see p. 62). However, the two colonies were more alike in their Puritanism than they were different in their way of understanding Church government.

VIRGINIA

The Virginia Company was formed in 1606 by some of the leading Puritan landowners of England, for the purpose of creating a trading and farming colony, especially for the raising of tobacco. The colonists arrived in April of the next year. The opening up of the North American forest for settlement was never easy. An English colony founded nearby in the previous year entirely disappeared, and a majority of the people who came over died in the first year, among them the minister. But a new group of immigrants arrived in 1610, including another minister.

From the beginning, Virginia was intended to be a Christian community, and the colony resembled Calvin's Geneva more than it did any English community. Every immigrant was required to apply for Church membership, and all adults had to attend church twice a day. Anyone cursing God was to be executed. Land was set aside for the support of the Church and the minister.

The colony was officially Anglican, but in fact it was tolerant of all forms of Puritanism in the earliest period. In 1610, as only one hundred of the original 775 settlers remained alive, the colony appealed to all dissatisfied Separatists to migrate to it.

PLYMOUTH

The second English settlement also came under the authority of the Virginia Company. In 1608 they had moved to the Netherlands, to avoid King James's attempts to enforce uniformity on the English Church. While they were there, the Virginia Company invited them to join its colony. Their experience under the tolerant Reformed Church of the Netherlands led them to relax their strict rejection of the official Church. They agreed to Seven Articles proposed by the Company, which included recognizing the legitimacy of the Church of England.

A third of these 'pilgrims' sailed to North America in the small ship *Mayflower*, which through an error in navigation, landed its 99 passengers, not in Virginia, but considerably to the north. They landed in what is today called Plymouth in Massachusetts on 21 December 1620. They arrived at the wrong time of year, and winter in Massachusetts is considerably more severe than it is in Virginia. By spring, half the colony was dead, including one half of the heads of households and all but three of the wives. The colonists did not mark the graves of their dead, so that the Amerindians would not know how few of them were left.

This Plymouth colony in Massachusetts had the opportunity to practise its Separatist principles without interference. A congregation was formed wherever a group of believers gathered to draw up a Church Covenant, or common agreement, setting forth the beliefs, form of worship, Church government, and discipline which they intended to practise. Each congregation was completely independent of any other. A newcomer had to 'own the covenant', that is, accept the principles laid down, and convince the congregation that he was truly converted.

The Plymouth Colony also was lucky enough to become politically independent. The charter from the government by which the land which the colony occupied was granted to the Virginia Company, was eventually transferred to the Colony itself. The Colony was governed by an agreement called the 'Mayflower Compact', which all the settlers had signed before they left the ship.

7.1 'These "Pilgrims" landed at Plymouth, at the wrong time of year' (p. 93).
As S. E. Brown's engraving records, winter in Massachusetts is severe.

THE MASSACHUSETTS BAY COLONY

The most influential of all the Puritan colonies was founded in 1630, south of Plymouth, in the area of what is today Boston, Massachusetts. The colonists there shared many of the convictions of their neighbours in Plymouth, but were of a higher social class. Most of them were from land-owning families, and their educational level was remarkably high. Many of the colonists and all of the ministers were graduates of Cambridge University. The new colonists felt the need for their own educated ministry. They quickly set up a printing press, and in 1636 opened Harvard College to train ministers.

Every settler in the Colony was required to accept the discipline of the Church and attend all its services. Only full Church members were allowed to vote in the Colony's elections, that is, to become full citizens. And becoming a full Church member was not easy. It was not only necessary to 'own the covenant', and to live an upright life in the judgement of the elders of the congregation. The most important requirement was that each candidate for Church membership had to stand up during a Sunday Church service and describe his personal religious experience. He had to do this in such a way as to convince the Church members that he had indeed repented his sins and experienced the mercy of God. Later, in some places, only a tenth of those who attended services were full members. Only full members could receive the Lord's Supper and become full citizens of both Church and state.

TWO 'TROUBLERS OF ISRAEL'

Among highly educated people, stimulated to think by daily sermons, and conscious of the opportunities for freedom on the American Continent, there were bound to be differences of opinion. Within the first ten years of its life, the Massachusetts Bay Colony expelled two of its most remarkable citizens for being too independent.

ROGER WILLIAMS

The first of these 'independents', Roger Williams (1603–1683) was a Cambridge graduate who became a pastor in Plymouth, and later in Salem, Massachusetts. He soon began to have serious doubts about the way things were done in the colony. Williams believed that no Church should be officially established by the government, but that in principle each Church should take care of its own affairs without government assistance or interference. He also raised a very serious question by declaring that the Colony had acted illegally and immorally in taking over land from the local inhabitants. He felt the Colony should give up its charter.

Williams was expelled from Massachusetts Bay, and after a hard winter in the forest, he settled further to the south, at what is now Providence, Rhode Island. There Williams established a new colony based on the principles of full liberty in religion and fair dealings with the Amerindians. During the English Civil War, Williams returned to England, and in 1644 Parliament granted him a charter for the new colony. He welcomed dissenters of all kinds to his colony, and liked to engage in vigorous theological debate with them. Williams himself ended his life as a 'Seeker', one who believed the true Church had not yet been revealed to the world.

ANNE HUTCHISON

The second dissenter in Massachusetts Bay suffered a more tragic fate. Anne Hutchison (died 1643) was sister-in-law to one of the Boston ministers, and arrived in the Colony in 1634. Perhaps her troubles would have been less if it had been customary at the time for women to be theologians. Because St Paul had taught that women should not speak in Church, she organized a theological discussion group of women, who met after the Sunday service.

In these meetings, Anne Hutchison developed a theological point of view which was later denounced as 'antinomian'. The word comes from the Greek words *anti* (against) and *nomos* (law). The term antinomian was first used against Lutherans who believed that those who had been justified by faith no longer needed to pay attention to the moral law at all, but were governed directly by the Spirit of Christ.

Anne Hutchison thought that the Boston ministers were teaching that salvation came by keeping a kind of legal contract with God, in which there was left no place for real faith or the grace of God. She said that they believed that prayer, belief, church attendance, and a moral life were guarantees of salvation. This took all the meaning out of justification as Luther and Calvin understood it. The Boston ministers, she thought, were teaching that people really were saved by their own religious works.

Anne Hutchison had raised a serious and continuing problem in the theology of the Puritans. The Puritans on the one hand based their theology on 'justification' as the Reformers taught it, but on the other hand they placed heavy emphasis on obedience and regularity and uprightness of life. Anne Hutchison was not allowed to continue the debate. A synod met in 1637, at which her brother-in-law first defended her, but the pressure was too great and he changed sides. She was expelled from the colony, and after many sufferings she and her children were killed by Amerindians in what is now New York, in 1643.

The questions raised by these two courageous prophets, Roger Williams and Anne Hutchison, are still being discussed today.

NEW ENGLAND PURITANISM

The colonists in what came to be called 'New England', i.e. the northern third of the English colonies on the Atlantic coast of North America, kept themselves informed about events in England. Parliament had instructed an assembly of theologians to revise the Thirty-Nine Articles, and in 1643 they completed the Westminster Confession of Faith. A synod met in Cambridge, Massachusetts, from 1646 to 1648, and adopted the Westminster Confession, with a number of changes, as their common basis of faith. The changes made were in those parts of the Westminster Confession which set forth the Presbyterian system of Church government (see pp. 62, 65). The new document, called the 'Cambridge Platform', contained what has become the standard expression of the 'Congregational' view of Church government:

> A Congregational Church is by the Institution of Christ a part of the Militant Visible Church, consisting of a company of saints by calling, united in one body by a holy covenant.

Elders had authority only in the congregation which called them, and did not help to govern other Churches, as in the Presbyterian system. Ministers, also, were ordained by the congregation which called them. Although each congregation was independent, they consulted together in a synod about common problems of faith, worship, Church government, and discipline. But the decisions of the synod were not binding. Each congregation was free to use them as they chose.

The worship of the New England Puritans was much simpler than the worship in the Reformed Churches of Europe. The service consisted of long prayers by the minister, Bible reading, and the singing of rhymed versions of the Psalms without any set tune. Each person believed for himself, and also sang whatever tune he liked, and the noise must have been terrific. The centre of the service was the sermon, which was usually an hour or sometimes two hours long. The preacher explained the text, then developed it doctrinally, and ended with an 'application' related to the actual problems of the congregation. We, today, might not find this very stimulating, but New England was a land without newspaper, radio, television, or theatre, or regular public amusements of any kind.

JONATHAN EDWARDS (1703–1758)

One of the important things about New England was that a highly educated people were building an entirely new life together with almost none of the usual circumstances of civilization. The New England theologians became known throughout the Protestant world, though the greatest of them was not born until the eighteenth century.

His name was Jonathan Edwards, born in Connecticut, a colony formed by people who moved South from Massachusetts Bay, and he was educated in the new Yale College, a rival to Harvard. He succeeded his grandfather as pastor in Northampton in 1729, and quickly became known as a major Christian thinker.

The Puritans believed that every Christian must have a real experience of conversion, and each pastor hoped that there would be a 'harvest', or time of general repentance, in his congregation. Edwards's grandfather had been famous for the several great 'harvests' which were experienced during his years in Northampton. Now Edwards discovered that his stern, logical, but vivid preaching about the justice of God and His sole claim on human life, was a powerful instrument for conversion. In 1734 a 'harvest' or revival, began in his Church, which lasted for more than a year. He wrote about it in a pamphlet which was read throughout the colonies and in England, and which led to a widespread revival throughout the colonies. This event, known as the Great Awakening, was at its height from 1740 to 1744.

The Great Awakening was violent in some of its forms. People cried out, shook, fainted, had hallucinations. Some experienced attacks of mental illness, and there were also suicides. There was considerable opposition as well as support in the Churches for this movement. Edwards discussed the movement in a series of theological works.

In a book whose short title is *Religious Affections*, Edwards declared that religion concerns people's whole lives, including their bodies. If we do not praise God with our emotions and bodies, he declared, we do not praise him at all. Therefore preaching and theology must reach people's emotions as well as their minds. Conversion means a new creation in which a person's entire life is changed, he comes to understand that what is good and right is simply God Himself. There can be no compromise between self-centredness and God-centredness. Therefore the line between the believer and the unbeliever must not be blurred. Only those who have experienced the converting love of God in a concrete way really 'own the Covenant', whatever their outward behaviour may be. According to this teaching, only the truly converted, whose lives are completely changed, may become Church members.

GROWTH OF DENOMINATIONALISM

By the end of the eighteenth century, the Churches in America showed three common characteristics which set them apart from the world Christian community as a whole:

1. They were Puritan,
2. They accepted the principle of a radical separation of Church and state,

3. They were properly called 'denominations', rather than Churches or sects.

'Puritanism' as used here, of course means something broader than the desire to purify the Church of England. This 'Puritan' outlook developed in its own way in New England, and influenced all Church life in the United States, even the Roman Catholic Church. Puritanism in this wider sense involved three basic commitments:

1. to the Bible as the sole source of saving knowledge,

2. to the responsible individual as God's instrument and the object of His suffering love, and

3. to society as the place where God's purpose is to be worked out. This Puritan view is very different from the ideas of medieval Christians, who believed that saving knowledge was to be found in the traditions and authority of the Church. Medieval Christians saw the individual person only in the context of his place in the social order, and regarded society itself as something given by God and unchanging.

This Puritan outlook was developed in New England in the seventeenth century. *Denominationalism* began to emerge in the eighteenth century, and was much influenced by the Great Awakening (see p. 98) The German social thinker, Ernst Troeltsch (1845–1923), divided Christian groups into 'Churches' and 'sects'. By 'Churches' he meant official state or 'established' Churches, and by 'sects' he meant the other Christian groups in countries with state Churches. This division fitted very well the Church situation in Europe after the Reformation, but it did not fit North American conditions at any period.

The Anglicans and Independents who founded most of the English colonies in North America all believed there should be a state Church. Five colonies eventually had established Churches of their own. But the American situation was not favourable to religious establishments. Many of the immigrants had come across the Atlantic to get away from oppressive authorities of that kind. They also came from many different religious backgrounds, and did not easily fit into a pattern of religious uniformity. As the population increased, people moved westwards to form new settlements, and this made it difficult to enforce rules of Church membership. People found that their shared experiences as emigrants and 'frontiersmen' were more important than their religious and national differences.

The Great Awakening had played an important part in this change, as preachers of various traditions travelled about, preaching more or less the same message. The important matter was not what Church you attended, but whether you were for or against the revival. Some Churches divided over this issue.

Political events also hastened the reshaping of Church life in America. As the split with England became deeper, the colonies were faced with the possibility of a single nation with five different 'established' Churches.

'Denomination' originally meant simply 'name', or the characteristic which distinguished one member of a species from another; what makes one Siamese cat different from another one. Benjamin Franklin in America and John Wesley in England were among those who helped give 'denomination' its current meaning in Church language. Denominations are Churches or groups of congregations which accept one another as more or less true to their common Lord, and which are entirely independent of any other Church or group. They strive that all shall have equal right before the law.

SOME AMERICAN DENOMINATIONS

The American denominations came from three sources:

1. Some came directly from Europe, and retained their original form, although all of them adapted in some ways to the American situation. This first group includes the Anglicans, Lutherans, Reformed-Presbyterian, Anabaptists, and of course the Roman Catholic Church.

2. Some arose from the sectarianism of the latter period of the English Civil War. In some cases these Churches were first formed in England, but reached their maturity in North America. These include Baptists, Quakers, and later Methodists (see pp. 115, 116).

3. Some were founded in America itself.

1. DENOMINATIONS ORIGINATING IN EUROPE

This first group will not be discussed in detail here (see p. 99).

2. DENOMINATIONS ORIGINATING IN ENGLAND

The English-speaking *Baptists* are not directly related to the European Anabaptists, although there have been contacts between them. The English Baptists developed out of a somewhat similar experience. Some of the Puritan Independents began to doubt that the Bible really taught the baptism of babies, and so they stopped the practice. English Baptists suffered considerable persecution, and produced a very notable writer, the lay-preacher John Bunyan, who wrote *Pilgrim's Progress* while in jail for unlicensed preaching. The Baptists, as Independents, were Congregational in their Church government, and adopted no common theological position. As a result, from an early period there were a number of Baptist bodies, most of them differing over theological teachings.

The Baptists proved an extremely suitable Church for the American frontier, where people lived at a distance from each other. Local congregations could be formed without the approval of distant Church authorities, and one member could be chosen as the minister without being tested by fellow-ministers. The Baptist Churches grew rapidly during the Great Awakening. By the middle of the nineteenth century they were the largest single Protestant group in the United States, and remain so today. Black slaves in America became Baptists in large numbers.

The *Quakers* were a small group, which began during England's 'Radical Reformation', the Civil War period. They were in some ways the most radical group of all, rejecting everything external and institutional in Christianity. Founded by a mystical shoemaker, George Fox (1624–1691), they believed that the Christian life was no more and no less than faith in Christ and obedience to the Inner Light of His Spirit. Anything added to this, they thought, was simply a corruption. Fox did not found a Church, but The Society of Friends, whose members refer to one another as 'Friends'. The nickname 'Quaker' referred to the intensity of their prayer and witness.

Traditionally Quakers practise a unique form of worship, the 'silent meeting'. The Quakers reject the ordinary names of the days of the week as pagan, and call the Sunday service the 'First Day Meeting'. They gather on Sunday in a group for an hour, simply sitting in silence until someone is 'moved' to speak, pray, or sing. Even weddings are performed in this way. At the end of the hour they arise and shake hands, and the service is over. There is no minister, nor do they use water, bread, or wine in the sacraments. Quakers, who have never been a large group, have always been noted for the earnestness and practicality of their social concern. They were among the first Christian groups to attack the institution of slavery, and they worked for prison reform and for world peace. Like the Anabaptists, Quakers do not swear oaths or become soldiers.

Quakerism had its greatest moment when King Charles II granted a large area of land in North American to William Penn (1644–1718), a prominent Quaker. Penn called his colony Pennsylvania, that is 'Penn's Woods', and called his capital *Philadelphia*, 'the city of brotherly love'. As long as Quakers controlled the colony, their relationships with the Amerindians were as good as in Roger Williams' Rhode Island. At first Pennsylvania maintained no army, and welcomed persecuted groups from Europe, including many of the Anabaptists, to become settlers.

3. DENOMINATIONS ORIGINATING IN AMERICA

While groups like the Baptists and Quakers began in Europe and achieved their maturity in America, other Christian denominations began in America itself. Some of the most important of these arose in the nineteenth and twentieth centuries. One which developed during the eighteenth century was not a denomination but a group of denominations using a common name, the 'Christian Church'. This confusing name arose from their rejection of denominational differences which were so apparent in America. Having experienced the revivals of the Western frontier territory, they believed that all Christians should reunite on the basis of a simple Biblical faith and form of Church life. Taking as their basis 'no creed but Christ,' they rejected confessions of faith, and adopted a simple form of worship based on the Book of Acts, with communion every Sunday, and congregational Church government. The largest of these groups is known today as the Christian Churches (Disciples of Christ).

THE WALL OF SEPARATION

Denominationalism thus grew up naturally among an immigrant people moving into new lands. One aspect of denominationalism is clearly expressed in the Constitution of the United States, as it was approved in 1787. This idea was later referred to in legal decisions as 'a wall of separation between Church and State'. This suggests something more radical than mere religious liberty. And this radical interpretation was increasingly emphasized as the American nation grew towards maturity.

The government was not to show favouritism, nor give legal recognition to any particular religious group. The idea itself had a long history in colonial America. Roger Williams of Rhode Island wrote in his tract, *The Bloody Tenet of Persecution*:

> Faith is that gift which proceeds only from the Father of Lights . . . and till he please to make his light arise and open the eyes of blind sinners, their souls shall lie fast asleep (and the faster, if the sword of steel compells them to worship in hypocrisy) in the dungeons of spiritual darkness and Satan's slavery.

But Roger Williams had few supporters in his own time. He was answered by John Cotton of Massachusetts in *The Bloody Tenet Washed in the Blood of the Lamb*, which defended established Churches. Williams replied to Cotton in *The Bloody Tenet Yet More Bloody*. But other forces in America were moving towards a separation of Church and state. The first was the fact of religious diversity; many of the denominations wished to become the established Church, but none would give place to another.

Another important factor was the attitude of leaders of the American Independence movement, such as Thomas Jefferson, Benjamin Franklin, and John Adams. They were followers of the new Rational Religion of England and France (see pp. 107 and 118), and believed that any restriction on religious belief, speech, or action was a violation of man's natural rights. They also believed that if men were let alone they would all become believers in that same Rational Religion.

All of these influences led up to the First Amendment of the United States Constitution, which begins 'Congress shall make no law respecting any establishment of religion, or prohibiting the free exercise thereof . . .'. Even before the Constitution was adopted, the views of American leaders on this matter were clear. The Pope was anxious to appoint a Vicar Apostolic to oversee the Catholic Church in America. The usual practice in other countries was for Rome to approach the government privately first, in order to find out what candidates might be acceptable. But in the United States this procedure did not work. Approaches were made to Benjamin Franklin, American ambassador to France, and also through the French ambassador to the United States, and directly by the Pope to the Continental Congress. But there was no satisfactory reply. The French ambassador remarked: 'The state legislatures and Congress refrain from entangling themselves in religious matters.'

At first this Wall of Separation was understood to mean that, although the United States was a Christian and Protestant nation, no particular denomination would be favoured or supported by the government. But later the increase in immigration from the non-Protestant parts of Europe brought about a more radical interpretation of the First Amendment: the government should not even favour the Christian religion, or indeed any religion at all. For this reason the American Supreme Court eventually ruled that prayers or Bible-reading in government-supported schools was illegal. For many Protestant Americans this attitude was a very bitter blow indeed.

STUDY SUGGESTIONS

WORD STUDY

1. What geographical region does the phrase 'New England' refer to?
2. What does the word *antinomian* mean?
3. What is the original meaning of the word 'denomination', and how is it used in the Church today?

REVIEW OF CONTENT

4. What regulations on religious life were in force in the Virginia Colony?
5. What was the Mayflower Compact?
6. What did a person have to do to become a Church member in the Massachusetts Bay Colony?

7. What did Roger Williams object to in the life of Massachusetts Bay?
8. What were Anne Hutchison's chief criticisms of the theology of the Boston preachers?
9. What was the Cambridge Platform?
10. Describe the worship of the American Puritans.
11. How did Jonathan Edwards understand conversion?
12. Why did Baptist Churches grow so rapidly on the American frontier?
13. Describe a Quaker 'silent meeting'.
14. What did the Wall of Separation separate?

DISCUSSION AND RESEARCH

15.(a) In some Churches every baptized child is a Church member. In Orthodox Churches they may even take communion. What should be required of someone who desires to become a member of a Church?
    (b) What is the status of a baptized child in your Church? If your Church does not baptize children, what is the status of a child of Church members?
16. Do you agree with Roger Williams that Churches should not receive special protection and attention from the government? What is the relationship of your own Church to the government? Do you feel the present arrangement is a good and helpful one? Give your reasons.
17. Read 1 Corinthians 1.10–17. Which of the American denominations described in this chapter seems to have been trying to obey Paul's teaching in this passage?
18. Read 1 Corinthians 14.33–36. Do you think those who condemned Anne Hutchison were right in their interpretation of Paul's meaning in this passage?
19. Find out as much as you can about Christian Churches and groups in your country or area, and how they originated. Which, if any, derive from the denominations described in this chapter? What are the relationships between them? What are the special relationships, if any, between them and the different social, political, or economic groups in the country. In what ways do you think these relationships help or hinder the spread of the Gospel?

CHAPTER 8

A 'Rational and Practical' Christianity

From 1530 to about 1690 Western Europeans were involved in a series of bitter and exhausting religious wars. In England, struggles over religion continued until the last Stuart King, a Roman Catholic, was overthrown in 1688. In 1685 the French King gave Protestants fifteen days to change their faith or leave the country. In the Holy Roman Empire, Roman Catholics, Lutherans, and the Reformed finally agreed to mutual toleration in 1648, after the Germans had suffered the bitterest religious conflicts of all. The religious wars in the Empire had ended in the Thirty Years War (1618–48), during which Germany was ravaged not only by its own Protestant and Catholic armies, but also by those of Denmark, Sweden, and France. During these wars the population of Germany declined from sixteen million people to six million.

European children today love the fairy stories collected by Jakob and Wilhelm Grimm. These stories, such as 'Hansel and Gretel' and 'Snow White', tell of wild animals, dangerous forests, wandering soldiers, and peasants who were so poor that they had to abandon their children. They accurately reflect the social background of the period in which they were told: the Germany of the Thirty Years War.

CHRISTIANITY AND PHILOSOPHY

By the end of the seventeenth century Europe was becoming prosperous again through trade and industry. Modern cities began to appear at this time throughout Europe. But life was dangerous, the poor suffered great hardships, and the political situation remained unstable. A few thoughtful men began to search for a new basis for a more peaceful and happy life for individuals and society. As they looked back through history all seemed dark, right back to the fall of the Western Roman Empire about the year 450. These men invented the phrase, 'the Middle Ages' to refer to everything which happened between the Roman period and their own. Humanism had much influence during this period (see p. 21). The earlier humanists collected Greek and Latin manuscripts. The humanists of the seventeenth and eighteenth centuries tried to copy the way of life of the ancient Greeks and Romans.

New ways of thinking were becoming accepted, chiefly in the field of science. In the seventeenth and eighteenth centuries 'science' chiefly meant mathematics and physics. The humanists and the new scientists

8.1 'New ways of thinking were becoming accepted, chiefly in the field of science' (p. 105).
King Louis XIV of France was a patron of science; Sebastien Leclerc's engraving shows the king visiting an observatory.

agreed that religion as it was practised at the time had not helped men very much, either to understand the world or to live a happy life. During the confusions of the Reformation, different standards of religious truth were argued, and during the Wars of Religion, men had killed each other in defence of different ways of knowing the will of God. Now some men tried to discover more certain and dependable ways to truth. One of them, the English philosopher John Locke, wrote:

> In all that is of divine revelation, there is need for no other proof but that it is an inspiration from God, for he can neither deceive nor be deceived. But how shall it be known that any proposition in our minds is a truth infused by God? . . . The strength of our persuasions is no evidence at all for their truth . . . men may be as positive . . . in error as in truth. (*The Dangers of Enthusiasm*)

Thinkers in the seventeenth and eighteenth centuries gave two different answers to the question: How can we have certain and dependable truth? These two answers arose from two different ways of learning and knowing things:

1. The *Rationalists* (from the Latin *ratio*, meaning 'reason') saw that the most certain kind of knowledge is mathematics. Truth, they said, consists of 'self-evident principles'—things which everyone naturally knows, organized into a logical system. Their model was geometry. Rationalism was especially popular in continental Europe.

2. The *Empiricists* (from the Greek *empeiria*, meaning 'experience') were those who believed that all real knowledge comes from common experience. Everything we know comes through our senses; sight, hearing, taste, touch and smell. Their example was the way a small child learns to speak. The most important empirical philosophers were English.

RATIONAL RELIGION

Christian thinkers who looked for a union of reason and faith in the seventeenth and eighteenth centuries turned to the Rationalism of continental Europe. They did this in three ways: (1) by defending Christian orthodoxy with rationalist arguments; (2) by remaking Christian theology to fit into rationalist philosophy; and (3) by replacing Christianity with a universal philosophical religion.

1. The first group included William Paley, author of *Evidences of Christianity* (1794). Paley constructed an argument which has become famous, to prove God's creation of the world. He wrote that if someone found a watch abandoned on a beach, he would have to conclude that somewhere there was a watchmaker. In the same way, Paley argued, the orderliness of the world proves the existence of a Creator.

2. The second group, those who tried to *remake* the Christian faith along more rational lines, included John Locke, who wrote a book called *Reasonableness of Christianity* (1695). Locke wrote that the existence of God and the rightness of Christian morals can be shown by human experience. The basic principles of religion can be defended by ordinary reason. What the Bible teaches goes beyond what we can prove or experience, but it does not contradict what we can know through our own experience.

3. The third group of rationalist theologians had a more lasting influence. These thinkers believed that they had discovered the most ancient and truest religion of all, which they called 'natural religion'. Men like Edward Lord Herbert of Cherbury (1583–1648) believed that among the ideas which are imprinted in the mind of everyone from birth are five religious truths, i.e.:

1. that there is a God;
2. that God should be worshipped;
3. that religion teaches the difference between right and wrong;
4. that we shall be punished for our sins; and
5. that there will be rewards for goodness in a future life.

Matthew Tindal well expressed the belief that this simple 'natural religion' is the real religion of all men, in the title of his book *Christianity as Old as Creation* (1730).

The idea of a 'natural religion' was quickly adopted by many thinkers in France and Germany. Some felt that this idea could be used to purify Christianity. Others regarded it as a replacement for Christianity. This second, more extreme group were called 'Deists', because they believed in God (Latin: *Deus*), but not in the Trinity nor in Jesus as our Redeemer. The Deists were most influential in France, where many were among the contributors to the *Encyclopaedia*, the immense work in many volumes intended as a complete review of literary and scientific knowledge. But the most famous writing by a Deist was a book by Thomas Paine, an Englishman who was a leader in the American struggle for independence, and later took part in the French Revolution. Thomas Paine (1737–1809) had a natural genius for making up titles, and the name of his book, *The Age of Reason* (1795), came to be used as a way of describing all of eighteenth-century European thought. Paine rejected much of traditional Christian teaching, and concluded:

It is certain that, in one point, all nations of the earth and all religions agree; all believe in a God; the things in which they disagree, are the redundancies annexed to that belief; and therefore, if ever a universal religion should prevail, it will not be by believing anything new, but in getting rid of redundancies, and believing as man believed at first. Adam, if ever there was such a man, was created a Deist. . . .

PIETIST CHRISTIANITY

THE REACTION OF PROTESTANT ORTHODOXY

About the middle of the sixteenth century, Protestant theology began to 'settle down'. It was clear by then that the separation of the Protestant Churches from the authority of Rome was going to continue. So Protestant theologians decided that it was necessary to set forth Protestant teachings in the same systematic and well-rounded way in which the medieval Scholastic theologians had expressed their theology. At the same time, both Lutheran and Reformed theologians were invòlved in a series of theological controversies, which made the problems more urgent and more complicated. The result was what historians call 'Protestant Orthodoxy', i.e. the formulation of official teachings in large volumes called 'Dogmatics' or 'Systematic Theology'.

In 1577 three Lutheran theologians drew up the *Formula of Concord*, a 300-page book setting forth the official view on no less than twelve theological controversies which had arisen among Luther's followers. The subjects ranged from how much compromise should be permitted in reunion discussions with the Roman Catholics, to the form in which Christ's body was present in the Lord's Supper.

The Reformed debated among themselves concerning the authority and the interpretation of the Bible, and the proper understanding of Calvin's teaching on predestination. All Lutheran Churches used the same statement of their faith, the Augsburg Confession (see p. 12), which was elaborated in the *Formula of Concord*. The Reformed, on the other hand, had separate confessions of faith for each national Church, such as the Gallican (or French) Confession and the Scots Confession.

In the seventeenth century, some Lutheran and Reformed congregations along the northern part of the Rhine River in Germany and the Netherlands began to protest against this exclusive concern of Church leaders with scholarly theology. These groups felt that the intense longing for a relationship with God with which the Reformation began was being lost. The region where this protest began had also been the centre of the German mystical movement which had begun in the fourteenth century, and which strongly influenced Luther himself. The most prominent leader in the early period of this protest was Philip Jacob Spener.

PHILIP JACOB SPENER (1635–1705) AND PIETISM

Spener was born in Alsace, the frontier land between France and

Germany, and was educted in the Reformed cities of Basel and Geneva, and in Strasbourg. He became a Lutheran pastor in Frankfurt, where he improved the catechism used to instruct children in the Christian faith. He also tried to apply Church discipline in his congregation, which was not usual in Lutheran Churches. In 1670 he organized a prayer group in his congregation, which he called a *collegium pietatis*, (Latin for a 'community of piety'). In 1675 he published a book which became the handbook of the movement, entitled *Pia Desideria* (Latin for 'Pious Desire'). The Pietist movement took its name from the title of this book.

To understand the protest of the Pietists, we must consider the situation of the German Lutheran Churches in the seventeenth and eighteenth centuries. The pastors were appointed and paid by the government. They had special government responsibilities, such as keeping local records, and were often considered to be police informers. These pastors were responsible to the rulers of the various German states, and the oversight of the Churches was the responsibility of the local government officials. Church activity itself was strictly limited to the Sunday service and the training of children for Church membership. Too much activity in the Church was regarded with suspicion. There were no theological colleges or seminaries as we understand them today. Pastors studied in the faculties of theology of the government universities, where their teachers might or might not be believing Christians. Compared to the situation of that time, all Churches today are 'pietistic'.

In his book *Pia Desideria*, Spener proposed that the Church should be renewed through 'little Churches within the Church', or, as we might say today, cell-groups. He agreed with Luther and Augustine that the true Church was always a small minority within the visible Churches, and under his leadership small groups of Church people met for Bible study and prayer. Spener insisted that these groups must always work to be leaven within the official Churches, and must not split off from them. He taught that Christianity means a renewed spiritual life, which must be shown through pious or holy behaviour: he declared that true Christians would not attend the theatre, dance, or play cards. Spener also experimented with new and simpler forms of worship, which could be altered to fit the needs of the congregation at a particular time, and he introduced regular periods of silent meditation into the Sunday service.

Perhaps the most controversial of Spener's ideas was his demand that only 'converted' university professors should teach theology. Theology, he said, was more a matter of the heart than of the mind, and nominal or 'unconverted' Christian professors could never teach true theology. This idea caused serious problems, since professors of theology were appointed and paid by the government, and were not in any way subject to Church control. This demand of Spener's led to one of the most important development of the Pietist movement: the establishment of the University of Halle.

THE UNIVERSITY OF HALLE

Spener's successor as leader of the German Pietist movement was August Hermann Francke (1663–1727), professor of theology at the University of Leipzig. Francke was less important as a theologian than as the organizer of Pietism. He founded Bible study groups among his students at Leipzig, and he himself experienced a conversion through them. After a visit to Spener, he too became convinced that professors of theology must be 'converted' persons. His views led the university authorities to expel him; and he was also dismissed from his next post at Erfurt.

Fortunately for Francke, the Elector of Brandenburg, who favoured Pietism, opened his own university at Halle, and appointed Francke to a professorship there. Under the influence of Francke and others, Halle became the centre of Pietist activities and influence. Under Francke's leadership, also, Pietists became noted for their very energetic benevolent activities. Francke founded an orphanage and a school for orphans, and established a printing press, and it was at Halle that the Great German 'Inner Mission' or home missionary association began.

But Halle is most famous in Church history as a training school for foreign missionaries. Halle did not itself send out missionaries, but it trained sixty German pietists as missionaries, who were sent overseas by British, Swiss, Dutch, and Danish missionary Societies. It is important to remember that the agencies established by the Pietists were never 'Church' agencies, since the official Churches did not engage in direct charitable or evangelistic work. The Pietist societies were independent bodies, supported by Christians on a voluntary basis.

NIKOLAUS VON ZINZENDORF (1700–1760)

Pietism became a truly international movement under the leadership of Spener's godson, Count Nikolaus von Zinzendorf. Zinzendorf, a nobleman from Saxony, was educated at Halle, and while he was there he experienced a Pietist conversion. He worked for the government of Saxony for a time, but he was always chiefly concerned for evangelism. The turning point in his career came when he agreed to allow a group of persecuted Bohemian Brethren to use a part of his estate as a refuge.

The Brethren were the descendents of a group of followers of John Huss (see Vol. 2, pp. 167, 168), who had developed a separate Church life in the province of Moravia. In 1620, after the first defeat of the

Protestants in the Thirty Years War, they were banned by the government. Some of these 'Moravians', however, managed, to keep their Church alive secretly for a hundred years. They accepted Zinzendorf's offer to build a community on his estate, and Zinzendorf himself reorganized the group in 1727 under the new name of the 'Unity of the Brethren'. They lived a strict and devout life, and were the first and most zealous of all Protestant foreign missionaries. Some of them went overseas as missionaries as early as 1732.

Zinzendorf wanted the Brethren to remain within the Lutheran Church, as a Pietist cell. But the differences and difficulties were too great. Zinzendorf himself was expelled from Saxony in 1736, and the next year he was consecrated bishop of the Brethren by a Reformed pastor in Berlin. After that his true career began. He visited the West Indies and North America, looking for places where immigrants could settle, and opportunities for evangelistic work. He created a community in Bethlehem, Pennsylvania, which is still well known for its German Church music. He began mission work among the Amerindians, and was among the first to work for a union of all German-speaking Protestants in Pennsylvania. This attempt was, however, unsuccessful.

Zinzendorf was largely responsible for encouraging the Pietists in a very passionate and personal relationship to Christ, and especially to the sufferings of Christ. A distinctive aspect of the Brethren's piety was their mystical devotion to the five wounds of Christ. This mystical devotion was closely united to a very practical organizing ability and concern for social welfare.

PIETISM AND METHODISM

JOHN WESLEY (1703–1791)

Pietism was introduced to the English-speaking world through the work of John Wesley, an Oxford graduate and High Church Anglican who was strongly influenced by the Moravian Brethren. Wesley was the son of an Anglican clergyman, and while at Oxford he and his brother Charles joined a group which met to study worship and the Christian life, and was commonly known by the nickname the 'Holy Club'. Under its inspiration, Wesley studied theology, and was ordained. He persuaded three other members of the group, including his brother, to join him in missionary work with the Amerindians in the English colony of Georgia.

Wesley's preaching and High Church ideas were not acceptable to the colonists, and after two years he 'ran away', as the official record put it. In Georgia, Wesley had come into contact with Moravians, and he went to them for spiritual guidance in his despondency after returning to England. It was at a meeting led by Moravians that

8.2 'Wesley agreed to take over an outdoor revival ... and was surprised at his own success' (p. 114).
William Hamilton's portrait of Wesley reflects his habit of outdoor preaching.

8.3 'Wesley's friend George Whitefield was the most famous of the travelling preachers of the Great Awakening' (p. 114).
In the engraving Whitefield is preaching to working people in Leeds.

Wesley for the first time experienced the peace of God's forgiveness.

In the following year, 1739, he most unwillingly agreed to take over an outdoor revival organized by his younger friend, George Whitefield. He was surprised at his own success, and as a result, decided to be a full-time evangelist. His real career had begun, and he continued to preach almost daily until his death more than fifty years later.

Wesley devoted his life to trying to revive the Church of England. His work was in every sense parallel to the Great Awakening in the American colonies (see p. 98). Wesley had been inspired by reading Jonathan Edwards's pamphlet on his revival in Northampton, and Wesley's friend Whitefield was the most famous of the travelling preachers of the Awakening. Wesley himself spent his life travelling about the British Isles, awakening Christian people to the meaning of the Gospel for their lives. There were two important differences, however, between what was happening in England and the Great Awakening in America:

1. The English revival was permanently identified with Wesley himself; he was far more prominent in it than Edwards was in the colonies.

2. The social consequences of Wesley's revival were as important as the religious ones.

Wesley preached his first revival sermon to miners, and he aimed his message especially at the working classes. After Belgium, England was the first country in Europe to become industrialized. Some of us know what it is like to move directly from an agricultural to an industrial society; but it is not very likely that we have experienced the full horror that this change brought to Europe. Today we are prepared by two hundred years of history to foresee some of the consequences of this change; but then everything was being tried for the first time.

The new labouring class in England worked without the right to vote, without labour unions, without factory laws, without the minimum standards of housing, health, and education required for human existence. It was places like Manchester and Birmingham in England that Marx and Engels used for examples in their writings, which formed the basis for the Communist movement. For English workers, industrialization meant a working day of twelve hours or more, child labour, a painful and empty life, and an early death.

On the whole, the workers were also without the Church. In England, as elsewhere in Europe, the Church was organized into parishes which had been linked to the centres of population in feudal and agricultural times. But the coming of the 'industrial revolution' caused large numbers of people to move suddenly to find work in the new factories. These factories were set up near the sources of raw materials or power, e.g. iron and coal mines. Entire new cities grew up before people had time to adapt to city life. The minister of a village parish might suddenly find himself responsible for a whole city.

This was the social background to Wesley's revival. He taught the new working classes how to live and what to live for. The immediate aim of the revival was to bring the estranged labouring classes back into an active Christian life, but the effects were wider than that. A social movement began which included a group known as the Evangelical (or Low Church) party within the Anglican Church. They worked for prison reform, factory legislation, a more representative Parliament, and an end to the slave trade around the world. This 'home mission' was so successful that of all the Labour or Socialist parties of Europe, only the one in England never adopted an anti-religious position.

THE METHODIST MOVEMENT

Wesley was a great organizer. He believed that the Christian life was not just a matter of being converted and then living happily ever afterwards. Christians need to 'grow towards perfection', or to a mature life of faith, and it takes a whole lifetime to do this. New converts in the revival were organized into 'classes', who met weekly, and took a pledge to live by a definite discipline. Attendance was checked at each meeting, and members were examined on their beliefs and behaviour. Admission to the class meetings was by ticket, and the ticket could be withdrawn from anyone who failed to keep the discipline.

At the same time, Wesley needed helpers in his work, so he appointed lay preachers to travel about preaching and visting class-meetings. He saw his work as administering a kind of home missionary society. But many Anglican Church authorities saw things differently. To them the annual conferences of Wesley's workers looked like the meetings of a synod in a diocese, and the resemblance became greater when the two 'superintendents', whom Wesley appointed to oversee evangelistic work in the American colonies, preferred to call themselves bishops. Wesley was censured by the Church of England for appointing ministers though not himself a bishop, and in 1795, four years after his death, the English Methodists organized themselves into a denomination. The American Methodists had been a separate denomination for some time, and became one of the strongest Churches in the colonies.

The name 'Methodist' was one of the nicknames which Oxford students used in order to make fun of the Holy Club. 'Bible Moths' was another. The term 'Methodist' stuck, because Wesley wanted Christianity to be understood as a 'way' or 'method' of life, involving discipline and organization.

Although Methodism may be referred to as a late-Puritan denomination, it is distinctive in its remarkably strong and centralized form of

Church government. The Methodist Church was first of all a missionary society, and its ministers were travelling preachers, called 'circuit riders'. They owed complete obedience to their District Superintendent and bishop, and could be freely moved from place to place. They did not serve a parish, but 'rode a circuit'. Many American Circuit Riders felt that it was necessary not to marry, and some literally worked themselves to death at an early age. Methodist bishops were considered to be the most powerful group of Church officials in the Protestant world.

STUDY SUGGESTIONS

WORD STUDY

1. Why was the term 'the Middle Ages' invented, and by whom?
2. From what language was the word 'Rationalist' derived, and what did the root word mean?
3. What Greek word lies behind the term 'Empiricist', and what does it mean?
4. Why were some believers in Natural Religion called 'Deists'?
5. Why were the followers of Wesley known as 'Methodists'?

REVIEW OF CONTENT

6. Why did the Reformation and the Wars of Religion which followed, lead some men to question the certainty of religious truth?
7. In what ways did the explanations of human knowledge given by the Rationalists differ from those given by the Empiricists?
8. Why were the Rationalists especially attracted to mathematics and geometry?
9. According to John Locke, where do our ideas come from?
10. What is meant by 'Natural Religion'?
11. What were the principles of Natural Religion, according to Lord Herbert of Cherbury?
12. What did the Pietists object to in the life of the Church in Germany in their time?
13. Describe some of Spener's reforms in his own congregation.
14. In what way was the University of Halle important for the Pietist movement?
15. What was the role of Zinzendorf in transforming the Moravian Brethren into the Unity of the Brethren?
16. List some of the special characteristics of Methodist Pietism.
17. Describe Methodist Church government.

DISCUSSION AND RESEARCH

18. Do you think that it is necessary to *prove* the truth of Christian

teachings? If so, how would you try to do this? If not, what sort of certainty or assurance must Christians have?

19. Is it possible to have a truly Christian life without believing all of the teachings of the Creed? Can you truly believe in God or in Jesus without believing in the Trinity, Original Sin, the Second Coming? Give reasons for your answers.

20. Do you yourself regard Christianity as a definite way of life? Do you think people should be able to recognize a Christian by the way he behaves? If so, what are some of the marks of the Christian life, and how do you recognize them? If not, what does Christian discipleship mean to you?

CHAPTER 9
Movements in the Roman Catholic Church

For Catholics, 'practical Christianity' meant bringing people to feel the power and meaning of the ceremonies and teachings of the Church. In the twentieth century this has been done by simplifying and translating the mass, so that it will 'come alive' in the congregation. In the earlier centuries it was done by providing special ceremonies and activities which would have a religious meaning for the people individually. These included saying prayers with the help of the rosary, or wearing articles which had been specially blessed, and new forms of devotional service, such as the adoration of the Sacred Heart of Jesus, or of the 'reserved sacrament' (i.e. the blessed communion bread left over after the mass).

Catholic theologians tried to answer those who argued for a Natural or Rational Religion for all men. But these centuries were not blessed with profound theologians. The best answer to unbelief was the lives of true believers. Although many things were wrong with the life of the Church in these centuries, it continued to produce saints, and these saints continued to nourish believers. Two good examples of the faith of the Church during this period were a Frenchman in the seventeenth century, and an Italian in the eighteenth century. Both were bishops who were declared to be saints—or perhaps it would be truer to say that both were saints who were made bishops.

TWO SAINTS

ST VINCENT DE PAUL

The Frenchman, Vincent de Paul (1580–1660), was born in a peasant family. After studying theology, he was captured by pirates, and lived the life of a slave in Tunisia for two years. He decided that the best way to express his faith, and to witness to the love of Christ, was to do charitable works among the unfortunate. Vincent lived for a time in the household of the General of the Galleys, who was in charge of the French warships. These ships were rowed by prisoners who were chained to their benches under the most miserable conditions. Vincent worked to relieve their miseries as much as he could.

Vincent's second idea was that any renewal of the Church must start from the renewal of the life of the local parish. He himself became famous for his work in rapidly bringing a neglected parish back to radiant Christian living. To make this work permanent, he founded

Vincent de Paul
Fondateur de la mission de S.ᵗ Lazare.

9.1   Vincent de Paul decided that the best way to witness to the love of
Christ was to do charitable works (p. 118).
Simon François' portrait, engraved by Edelink, gives us an idea of Vincent's
loving nature.

two new religious orders. The first, founded in 1625, was commonly known as the *Lazarists*. This was an order of priests (or Regular Clerks, see p. 68) whose two main tasks were to train priests, and to conduct 'missions' in country parishes.

'Missions' were a popular and important form of religious activity during this period. They were rather like the 'revivals' held in America in the nineteenth century. A famous 'missioner' was St Paul of the Cross, who founded the Passionist order. His method was to build a large platform in a Church or public place, with a large wooden cross set on it. There he preached every day for fifteen or twenty days, lashing himself with a whip, and finally leading his audience in a dramatic procession to the foot of the cross. St Paul of the Cross popularized the meditation on the fourteen 'Stations of the Cross'. For this, pictures or sculptures were set up around the walls of the church, representing the events of Jesus's walk to Golgotha. Believers walked from one Station to the next, praying before each. St Paul himself set up these Stations in hundreds of churches.

The other religious order, which St Vincent founded in 1633, was the *Sisters of Charity*. This order consisted of 'religious sisters' who did not remain in their convent, but went out to care for the poor and sick. Many Church people were offended by the sight of sisters wandering about in the world, but they made a great witness for the caring love of God for his people. Vincent was a royal counsellor to the French King Louis XIV during his boyhood, and organized relief work during the civil wars which occurred during that period.

ST ALPHONSUS LIGUORI

The Italian saint was Alphonsus Liguori of Naples (1696–1787). He belonged to a noble family, and was very brilliant. He became a Doctor of Law at the age of 16, and had an impressive legal career. But it happened that he lost a case as a result of confusing the law of two different Italian states, and this led him to reconsider the purpose of his life. He joined a religious order, and through this work learned of the horrifying conditions in which many people of Naples were living. He founded an order, the Redemptorists, to conduct missions among the poor to proclaim Christ who came to redeem the poor and lowly. St Alphonsus was a very dramatic 'missioner' himself, and used to preach on the Four Last Things (Death, Judgement, Hell, and Heaven), holding a skull in his hand and standing by a grim painting of the sufferings of the sinner in hell.

But despite his style, Alphonsus did not preach terror and judgement. Instead he taught 'confidence in God' (1 Peter 1.21), the God who is always ready to be merciful. He was influenced by the Jesuits, and wrote a famous book called *Moral Theology*, which continues to influence Catholic ideas about ethics. Alphonsus taught that receiving the sacraments was the basis of the Christian life, which is to be lived in dependence upon God's grace. Therefore, he said, the Church should be careful not to discourage its people by too harsh discipline, which would keep them from frequent communion. Priests should always take a very charitable view of sins, and encourage the sinner to repent and receive the sacrament again.

On a visit to the country districts of Southern Italy, Alphonsus was shocked to see the physical and moral life of the peasants there, which was much worse than what he had experienced in Naples. His concern led him to become bishop of a new and very poor diocese, and to devote himself to its renewal. In the latter part of his life he was crippled with rheumatism, and had to devote himself mainly to writing. He wrote works encouraging devotion to the Virgin Mary and the Sacred Heart of Jesus. Alphonsus was always a most obedient son of the Church. As he lay dying he was informed that, because of groundless jealousy, the Pope had condemned his order of Redemptorists. The dying man is said to have responded: 'The Pope's will is God's will. Lord, I wish all that you wish, I desire only what you desire.'

JANSENISM

Although the seventeenth and eighteenth centuries were not notable for development in theology, some theological controversies did occur. The most important of these arose when *Cornelius Jansen* (1585–1638), director of the theological college at Louvain, in what is now Belgium, began to oppose the theology of the Jesuits. In order to construct a strong theology which would effectively silence the Protestants, Jansen read the complete works of Augustine (see Vol. 1, pp. 126, 127, 129) ten times, and Augustine's writings against the Pelagians thirty times. After this preparation, he wrote a theological book called *Augustinus* in Latin.

Jansen learned from Augustine a broad and deep understanding of the meaning of faith. To have faith, as he understood it, was something entirely different from believing what the Church taught. Jansen also shared Augustine's deep horror of sin, and took a very serious view of the meaning of repentance. None of this fitted in well with the 'practical' religion, which the Jesuits were teaching in order to make belief and participation in the sacraments as easy as possible for lay people.

More serious than this, Jansen also took from Augustine's teaching about grace, the idea that God alone decides to whom He will be gracious. According to this teaching, Church members receive God's saving grace through the sacraments only if God wills that they should do so. Grace is not something which people can gain automatically as a result of performing certain actions. For Augustine, and for Jansen,

God's will and free graciousness towards us could not be understood in any other way. But the problem for both theologians was that this belief makes the salvation of faithful Church members quite uncertain. It also means that Church membership is not necessary for salvation.

It was Jansen's French associates and followers who spread his teaching and created the Jansenist movement, which flourished after his death. Jansenism became widely accepted because of the feeling among Catholic intellectuals that the theology of the Catholic Reformation lacked the seriousness and depth of the thought of the Protestant Reformers. The movement also included those who opposed the Jesuits for other reasons, and it was protected by those political leaders who resented the Jesuits' efforts to bring the Church in every nation directly under the control of the Pope. The two most important of the later Jansenist writings were (a) the *Provincial Letters* of Blaise Pascal, the most profound Catholic thinker of the period, in which he made fun of the Jesuits, and (b) the *Moral Reflections on the New Testament* by Pasquier Quesnal.

The chief stronghold of Jansenism was the convent of Port-Royal, near Paris. Pascal's sister was a nun there, and a miraculous healing of his sister's eye-disease strengthened Pascal's own faith. Her eye was exposed to a thorn, supposedly taken from the Crown of Thorns, which was in the possession of the French kings. Those associated with Port-Royal held a deep and serious view of the Christian life. They felt that it was proper to take the Lord's Supper only after a period of serious self-examination, and that it was better not to take it too often.

Catholic leaders began attacking Jansenism from an early date. They resented both its teachings and the stubbornness and independence of its leaders. The Jansenists were able to resist for a time, but Port-Royal was closed, and its nuns dispersed, and in 1713 the Pope condemned certain teachings in Quesnal's *Reflections*. The Jansenists refused to submit, and were also condemned. In 1723 a group of Dutch Jansenists were able to elect a Jansenist bishop of Utrecht. The Pope, of course, did not recognize this election, and the result was a small schism. The Jansenist Church continued as an independent body until it merged with a new schism in 1873, and formed the Old Catholic Church which continues today. It was two and a half centuries before the Catholic Church regained the theological depth which it lost in condemning Jansenism.

GALLICANISM

As we have seen, relationships between the Catholic Church and the various nations of Europe became increasingly tense during the seventeenth and eighteenth centuries. The Catholic nations, including the small states of Italy, demanded almost as much freedom from Church control as Henry VIII of England did in the sixteenth century. The extreme expression of this attitude in the seventeenth century was known as 'Gallicanism'. The name Gallicanism was used to mean religious nationalism in France, which was known to the Romans as 'Gaul' (Latin: *Gallia*).

From the time of the Great Schism of 1378 (see Vol. 2, p. 165), French theologians had maintained that the French king held a special position within the Catholic Church. This was because the early French kings had protected the Popes against the Arian Lombard tribes (see Vol. 2, pp. 59, 60). In the seventeenth century this special position was made clear in the four 'Gallican Articles', also known as the 'Gallican Liberties', which were composed by theologians of the University of Paris, and adopted by the French clergy in 1682. According to these Articles:

1. Kings were not subject to the Church in political matters.
2. The special rights of the French Church could not be changed.
3. Councils were superior to the Pope.
4. The judgement of the Pope was final only if it was affirmed by a Council.

These were, of course, very extreme ideas within the Catholic Church. It is not certain that they were meant to be taken entirely seriously. They were adopted at a time when the French king, Louis XIV, was quarrelling with the Pope over the appointment of some bishops. But most of the French priests agreed with them, and they were taught in the seminaries, although condemned by the Pope in 1690. They were finally withdrawn in 1693, but the spirit of independence which the Gallican Liberties represented remained alive in the French Church. The Jansenists appealed to them, and Gallican ideas have continued to be influential in the French Church down to our own time.

The opposing view was *ultramontanism,* from a Latin phrase meaning 'beyond the mountains'. This referred to the Alps, which separate France from Italy, the land of the Pope. Ultramontanism is the belief that the Pope has supreme authority over the Church throughout the world; i.e. his authority stretches 'beyond the mountains'. No Catholic really doubted that the Pope's word was final in theological matters; the disagreement concerned the administration of Church affairs. The Church was a large landowner, and thus had great political power in each nation. The Pope appointed bishops and archbishops, but did this give him the right to decide directly what they should do in their own territory? Each of the major Catholic nations had, over the centuries, developed its own traditions and ways of doing things, in some cases even in the liturgy. So people began to ask whether the life of the Church really had to be exactly the same everywhere.

SUPPRESSION OF THE JESUITS

The Jesuits, who represented the most lasting renewal of the Church since the Reformation, had gained many enemies just because of their successes. They were a new order, and a powerful one. The sons of the nobility were trained in their schools all over Europe. Jesuits were confessors to kings and powerful noblemen, and they engaged in commerce on a large scale through their lay members. The Franciscans and Dominicans, as well as the kings of Portugal and Spain with their rights under the *padroado* (see p. 81), were angry about Jesuit missionary practices in China and India (see pp. 84, 85). The Jansenists, of course, opposed them. But the chief enemies of the Jesuits were all those who opposed ultramontanism, both theologians and rulers. Some accused the Jesuits of teaching that a ruler who did not obey the Pope might be assassinated.

In 1759 the Jesuit order was suppressed in Portugal and the Portuguese territories. The Portuguese Church leaders were angered by the loyalty of the Amerindian villagers in Paraguay and Uruguay to their Jesuit protectors. Jesuits were also accused of taking part in an assassination attempt against the king, and one member of the order, over eighty years old, was burned to death.

In France there was a court case about a financial scandal in a company controlled by the Jesuits. A legal ban against the activities of the order in France was applied in 1764. Spain, who was a political ally of France, suppressed the Jesuits in 1767. In 1773 Pope Clement XIV suppressed the order throughout the Church. This decision was taken reluctantly, under heavy diplomatic pressure from Spain and France.

Curiously enough, this was not the end of the Jesuits. Independent Austria, Protestant Prussia, and Orthodox Russia did not recognize the Pope's decision. New members of the order were trained in Russia. Almost all the Catholic clergy in the United States, including the bishop, were Jesuits, and they simply continued working as ordinary secular priests. In any case, the Pope's decree was revoked in 1814.

But the effect at the time was still immense. The French Deist philosopher Voltaire was said to have laughed loudly at the news, and to declare: 'In twenty years there will be nothing left of the Church.' And much suffering resulted. The People of the Guaraní tribe, in what is today Paraguay and Uruguay, were slaughtered by neighbouring Spanish landowners who wanted their land and resented their superior position. Missions everywhere were disrupted as the order's activities came to an end. This was especially unfortunate as the rate of evangelism in foreign missions was slowing down anyway. In Europe the Church lost prestige and able leadership just at a moment of great crisis.

THE STATE OF THE CHURCH

The Roman Catholic Church at the end of the eighteenth century was not on the verge of death, as Voltaire and other 'enlightened' thinkers believed and hoped. The great masses of the people, a large majority of all Europeans, remained faithful Catholics. Missions around the world continued to grow, although more slowly than before. Many Catholics of this period were later declared to be saints. Churchmen laboured with some success to make the faith more directly meaningful to the people.

On the other hand, tensions between the Church and national governments continued to grow. There was a great gap between the bishops and other higher clergy, on the one hand, who were mainly from noble families, and the local priests, who were mostly from peasant families and sometimes very badly paid, on the other hand. Some high Church officials did not believe their own teachings. A Catholic historian cites a report which stated that 100 of the 135 French bishops were believed to lead moral lives, and this was considered to be a good average.

But the life of faith and devotion continued, and survived the painful testing of the French Revolution at the end of the century.

STUDY SUGGESTIONS

WORD STUDY

1. What does the word 'Gallican' mean?
2. What is the literal meaning of 'Ultramontanism', and how is it used in Church history?

REVIEW OF CONTENT

3. What problem did the 'national idea' raise for the Roman Catholic Church?
4. How did the Church try to make the faith more meaningful to lay people?
5. What was the special concern of St Vincent de Paul?
6. What were 'missions' in the Catholic Church?
7. What was the important teaching of the *Moral Theology* of Alphonsus Liguori?
8. Why was Jansenism condemned by the Church?
9. Why were the Jesuits suppressed?
10. What were some consequences of the suppression of the Jesuits?

DISCUSSION AND RESEARCH

11. The suppression of the Jesuits and the death of Vincent de Paul remind us that religious orders in the Catholic Church can compete

with each other, as some Protestant denominations do. In your own congregation there are probably differences and tensions between members. How do you as a Churchman think the Church should deal with differing understandings about Christian faith and life?

12. In chapters 8 and 9 we have studied ways in which Protestants and Catholics tried to make the faith more practical and meaningful. What is your opinion of these attempts? In what ways, if any, does your own Church try to make the Christian life more meaningful? Do these examples from history suggest any new possibilities to you?

CHAPTER 10

Asian and Orthodox Christianity

Since the Reformation, Europe has been the most influential centre of Christian life and activity. Until quite recently the leading theologians, the chief Church administrators, and the originators of ecumenical activity have mostly been Europeans, or men of European descent. Today the picture is changing, and as early as the year 1800, important centres of Christian activity had appeared in three other continents: South America, North America, and Asia. In this chapter we study the Church as it develops in Asia. The story begins with the events described in chapter 6, which should be kept in mind while reading this chapter.

INDIA AND CEYLON

During the three centuries which followed the Reformation, both Catholic and Protestant Churches were firmly planted in India. The ancient Syrian Orthodox community in South India also continued its life, although amid difficulties. To see the picture in perspective, however, we must remember that Islam, introduced by the Moghul Empire in North India, grew more quickly and strongly in the Indian sub-continent than the Church did. The Taj Mahal, memorial to a Muslim princess, became a world symbol for Indian culture, though India was and continues to be an overwhelmingly Hindu society. The Christian minority never assumed the leadership in society and government, in India as it did in some other Asian countries.

We have already described the beginnings of Roman Catholic missions in the Portuguese *padroado* (see p. 81). Hinduism was forbidden in the Portuguese colony of Goa, and by the end of the century almost the entire population there was Christian. There were also contacts between the Jesuits and the Moghul emperor, though they had no permanent results. The emperor Akhbar invited Julian Pereira to reside in his court about 1576. A church was built in Lahore, and the emperor permitted his subjects to become Christians. Only a few did so, however, and the attempt came to an end in the eighteenth century when the Jesuits were suppressed.

At the beginning of the seventeenth century in South India, however, Francis Xavier had a worthy successor in *Roberto de Nobili*. De Nobili was an Italian nobleman, and nephew to Cardinal Bellarmino. He arrived in South India as a Jesuit missionary in 1605, and quickly came to the conclusion that two things were hindering evangelism there:

(a) the Indians' hatred of the Portuguese invaders, and (b) the mission-aries' refusal to observe caste distinctions. De Nobili decided that it was necessary to become a Hindu in order to win Hindus. He dressed as a holy man, did not eat meat, and broke all contact with the existing Church and missionaries. In front of his Indian-style house he placed the following notice:

> I am not a *Parangi* ('Frank' meaning invader, i.e. Portuguese), I was not born in the land of the *Parangis* nor ever connected with their race . . . I came from Rome, where my family hold the same rank as respectable Rajahs do in this country. . . . The law which I preach is the law of the true God, which from ancient times was by his command proclaimed in these countries by holy men and saints. Whoever says that it is the law of the *Parangis*, fit only for low castes, commits a very great sin, for the true God is not the God of one race, but the God of all. . . .

De Nobili studied the local Tamil and Telugu languages, and was perhaps the first Westerner to master the classical Sanskrit language. He wrote and held discussions with Indian holy men, and with high-caste Brahmins. He wanted to show the universal truth of Christianity, and he taught that although the Gospel is a higher religious truth than the Hindu scriptures, a man can accept the Gospel without giving up what is true and valuable in Hindu culture.

We may imagine the feelings of the other missionaries, especially the Portuguese, when they heard of de Nobili's notice. For a time he was forbidden to work in Goa, and a complaint against him was sent to Rome. But during his lifetime the Pope supported him. De Nobili converted six hundred Brahmins to Christianity. For the first time, highly placed persons in a major Asian culture and religion were taking the Christian message seriously. De Nobili arranged for other Jesuits to work among the lower castes, and through their work a mass movement began, which by 1703 claimed 200,000 converts.

After the beginning of the eighteenth century, work in South India slowed down. This partly resulted from difficulties with the Portuguese authorities. There was no archbishop in Goa for twenty-three years. Another problem was the continuing controversy over de Nobili's methods. The separation of castes within the Church was condemned by the Pope, along with other 'Malabar Rites', in 1744. However, progress continued in north east India, in Bengal and around Calcutta. Indian priests were trained, Indian bishops appointed, and Christian literature was made available in seven Indian languages. By 1800 there were perhaps a million Roman Catholics in India.

A new beginning had also been made in 1793, with the arrival in India of the Baptist William Carey, who developed a far-ranging missionary programme, paving the way for the rapid advance of Protestant missions in the following century.

The *Syrian Orthodox Church of Malabar* (see Vol. 1. pp. 112–113) at first co-operated with the Portuguese against the Muslim threat represented by the Moghul Empire. This relationship reached its high point at the Diamper Synod of 1599, when the Syrian Church submitted to Rome and condemned the errors of Nestorius. The Church was reorganized, and a year later received a Portuguese Jesuit as bishop. The high-handed and insensitive methods of the Portuguese, however, soon alienated many people from this new Uniat church (see p. 14), and the Syrian Orthodox Church continued as an independent, but much smaller Church. Then a strange thing happened. Having no bishop to ordain their clergy, the Syrian Christians renounced their Nestorian allegiance and submitted to the Jacobite Patriarch of Antioch. Thus they moved from one 'anti-Chalcedonian' standpoint, the Nestorian, to the other, the Monophysite (see Vol. 1, p. 141). Having believed, as Nestorius did, that Christ is two complete 'persons' in one body, they now affirmed, as Cyril of Alexandria did, that Christ has only one, divine 'nature'. The Carmelite order continued to win individuals back to allegiance to Rome, and by the middle of the seventeenth century the Syrian Christians were divided into three Churches, Jacobite, Uniat (using the Syriac rite), and Catholics (using the Latin Rite).

Pietist missionaries from Halle (see p. 111) also began *Protestant mission work* in the Danish settlement at Tranquebar in 1706, with support from the recently founded (1698–9) British Society for Promoting Christian Knowledge.

Ceylon too had been dominated by the Portuguese, after they had erected a fort at Colombo in 1505. The king of Jaffna invited Franciscan missionaries, who baptized two of his sons. In 1658 the Dutch expelled the Portuguese, at which time the Franciscans and Jesuits claimed some 90,000 converts. The Dutch tried to stamp out both Buddhism and Catholicism from the island, and to develop a Reformed Church, but none of these attempts was very successful. In 1722 the Dutch claimed 420,000 Protestants, but they were cared for by only five pastors, only one of whom could speak a local language. The Catholic Church continued to grow through local priests working in secret, and Buddhism also experienced a revival.

THE SOUTH-EAST ASIAN MAINLAND

Malacca was the first centre of Christian predominance on the southeast Asian peninsula. But the Portuguese lost control there in 1641, and were succeeded by the Protestant Dutch and English, who did not engage in extensive evangelism. The most successful area of Catholic work was what later came to be called Indo-China, where Jesuits from Japan established themselves in 1615. Later, the French established a missionary society of 'secular' priests, i.e. priests who were not also members of religious orders, called the *Société de Missions Etrangères de Paris*, or Paris Mission. By 1786 there were 130,000 Christians in the province of Tongkin alone. Later missionary authorities arranged for the French government to support the exiled king of the region, and so helped to lay the foundations for French colonialism there.

At the same time, both the Portuguese and the Paris Mission made small beginnings in *Thailand*, where a training centre for national clergy was established. Portuguese missionaries made repeated attempts to work in *Burma*, a strongly Buddhist country, but without success.

THE 'EAST INDIES'

During this period the East Indies were no longer ruled by the Portuguese, but by the Dutch. The term 'East Indies' was used to include South India, Ceylon, and Indonesia, but here we shall only use it to mean what is now Indonesia. In exchange for a monopoly of navigation and trade from the Cape of Good Hope to the Straits of Magellan, the Dutch East India Company was required to carry out all the functions of government, including the 'spiritual' functions which were usual at that time, i.e. providing ministers and organizing a Church. The second charter of the United East India Company required it to:

care for the holy Church and oppose and eliminate all forms of idolatry and false religion, to destroy the kingdom of the Antichrist and promote the kingdom of Jesus.

At that time Protestants regarded the Roman Catholic Church as a part of the kingdom of Anti-Christ! So the 30,000 Catholics who had remained in the Moluccas through Muslim persecution were forced to become Protestants.

Under the terms of its charter, the United East India Company set up the Church of the Indies, a kind of 'company Church'. All employees of the Company were required to become Church members, and between 1602 and 1799, when the Company was dissolved, it had trained and sent out 254 ministers and 800 Sick-Visitors. The first pastors arrived in Ambon in the Moluccas in 1612, and in Kupang on Timor in 1670. By the end of the Company's life there were eighteen congregations in Indonesia. The entire Church of the Indies was led by a single governing board in Batavia (now Jakarta). The Governor General of the Indies was chairman, and two political commissioners were required to be present at each meeting. All correspondence was read and approved by the Governor General before being forwarded to the Church authorities in the Netherlands. This practice continued until 1935. A real 'Protestant *padroado*' was in effect.

Services were held in the Malay or Indonesian language from early times, but the Indonesian members of the Church never had equal status with the Dutch members. The Church was a careful copy of that in the Netherlands. Indonesians who agreed to be baptized were paid, and payment was also made to their local rulers and to the baptizing pastor. The New Testament was published in Malay in 1668, and the entire Bible in 1733.

A major problem which continued throughout the whole period was the lack of pastors. This lack gave the Church its special character. The vast majority of pastors at any one time were located in Jakarta. One congregation, located about a hundred miles from Jakarta was visited by a pastor only three times in fifty years. Services were conducted by local Indonesian 'congregational teachers', who used printed prayers and read from a book of printed sermons. One of the effects of this situation was that most baptized people never became full Church members, and many Christians were never legally married, since only ordained ministers could confirm and marry. In 1705 on the island of Sanghir, out of 3,298 baptized persons, none had been confirmed. The Dutch pastor there did not preach, since he thought it would be a waste of time.

Only one ordained Indonesian pastor worked in Indonesia during the entire two hundred years of the Company's life. In 1727 there were in Indonesia 55,000 baptized people, 1,200 full members, and 120 unordained Indonesian Church workers.

THE PHILIPPINES

We have already mentioned the beginnings of the evangelization of the Philippines (see p. 88). The main group of Filipinos had become Christian before the end of the eighteenth century. There remained some animist peoples in mountainous northern Luzon, and Muslims in the south. Spain abandoned its forts on the island of Mindanao and the Sulu Archipelago in the extreme South, and these regions were dominated by Muslims, whom the Spanish called 'Moros'. They remained a separate group, and today there is something like a civil war between the 5 per cent Moro minority and the Philippine government.

Although the evangelization of the Philippines was one of the most successful chapters in the history of modern missions, two major problems arose, which hindered its final success. The first was the reluctance of the religious orders to turn over their work to 'secular' clergy, i.e. bishops and regular parish priests. The bishops, and often the governor, tried to organize the Church into regular dioceses, but were frustrated by the powerful missionary orders.

This problem was related to the second one: the reluctance of the orders to ordain Filipinos to the priesthood. Father Gaspar de San Augustin wrote about 1720:

The Filipino's pride will be aggravated with the elevation to so sublime a state as the priesthood; their avarice with the increased opportunity of preying on others, their sloth with their no longer having to work for a living, their vanity with the praise they will seek, desiring to be served by those whom in another state of life they would have to respect and obey . . . For the Filipino who seeks holy orders does so not because he has a call to a more perfect state of life, but because of the great and almost infinite advantages which come to him along with the new state of life he chooses. How much better to be a Reverend Father than to be a farmer or labourer! What a difference between paying tribute and being paid a salary! Between being drafted to cut timber and being waited on hand and foot! Between rowing a galley and riding in one!

(Quoted from Peter G. Gowing, *Islands Under the Cross*)

As the orders held this quite mistaken view of the capabilities of the Filipino people for the priesthood (and a very curious view of the priesthood itself), it is not surprising that they wanted to keep the priesthood in the hands of the Spanish friars, and that training for the priesthood was slow to begin. When Spanish control of the Philippines ended, in 1899, there was not a single Filipino bishop.

CHINA

The great empire of China was a very important field for the Christian mission to Asia. The Chinese emperors ruled over more people than the whole population of Europe and the Americas combined. One of the Jesuits who was attached to the Moghul court in India, proved, by walking from North India to the borders of China via Turkestan and Tibet, following the route of Marco Polo, that China was indeed the land which Marco Polo had called 'Cathay'. He died before reaching his Jesuit colleagues in Peking, and one of them remarked that he 'looked for Cathay and found heaven'.

Although Francis Xavier also had died before reaching China, his Jesuit successors were working in the land he did not live to see. The Portuguese controlled Macao, which the Jesuits used as their base for the China mission. The first entry was made by Michael Ruggieri and

Matteo Ricci in 1582 (see Vol. 2, p. 80). Ruggieri himself left after a few years to try and get European support for the China mission. Ricci proved a worthy successor to Francis Xavier, and was perhaps the inspiration for Roberto de Nobili's work in India a little later.

Matteo Ricci was an Italian, like de Nobili, and was born in Northern Italy in 1552. He studied mathematics and astronomy in Rome, and then went on to Goa for his theological studies. In 1583 the Chinese authorities gave Ricci and Ruggieri permission to live near Canton. There Ricci entertained visitors by showing them mechanical clocks and a world map which he had drawn, with the 'Middle Kingdom' of China at its centre. Like de Nobili, Ricci tried to attract the upper classes as the beginning of evangelism. But they were not the only converts; unlike India, China had no caste system, and Ricci baptized a poor beggar who became his companion. In 1594, perhaps to make themselves less conspicuous, Ricci and two other Jesuits dressed themselves as Buddhist monks. But they soon discovered that monks had a very low place in Chinese society, so they changed their dress again for that of Confucian scholars.

One very special characteristic of the government in China was the system of examinations in the Confucian classics. Chinese society was highly centralized, and all power was held by the higher ranks of imperial officials. To become an official it was not necessary to be of noble birth, nor to be rich, although these helped. One had to be successful in passing examinations in China's classical Confucian literature. In this way, a scholar from the lower classes might become prime minister. This class of scholar-officials was very conservative, and viewed the new teachings of Christianity with deep suspicion. Since learning was the gateway to power, foreign learned men of another religion and social system were looked upon as a great threat to the Chinese way of life.

Jesuits like Ricci were successful because they accepted the position of the Confucian scholars, and because of their skill in the mathematical sciences and in engineering, which had declined in China. They were known as mathematicians and astronomers. A Chinese chronicler noted approvingly that Ricci wrote many books on subjects on which no Chinese had yet written. Like de Nobili, Ricci distinguished between Chinese customs and practices which were specifically religious, and those which were primarily cultural or civil, and permitted his converts to continue practising the latter. Since Chinese religion was quite different from the other widespread religions, Ricci adopted Chinese terms, which he thought would convey the right idea of God to the Chinese mind. He called God either *T'ien*, meaning 'heaven' (as in 'Kingdom of Heaven'), or *Shang-ti*, meaning 'high Lord'.

In 1598 Ricci was permitted to move to Nanking, where he converted

10.1 'Jesuits like Matteo Ricci were successful in China because they accepted the position of Confucian scholars' (p. 133).
The engraving shows Ricci with Ly Paulus, a Chinese 'propagator of Christian law'.

the first government official, who was baptized as Paul Hsu. The Hsu family have remained prominent Catholics down to the present. In 1601 Ricci at last received permission to move to Peking, the imperial capital. There the Emperor gave him a house and a salary. By 1605 he had 200 people studying the Christian faith. When he died, in 1610, Ricci was buried in Peking in Chinese style.

The year after Ricci's death the Jesuits in Peking were put in charge of the official calendar. Adam Schall von Bell became famous for correctly predicting an eclipse which the Muslim astronomers had miscalculated. There were some minor persecutions during this period, but as a favour to Schall (see p. 136), the Emperor proclaimed toleration, and built a Church in Peking. By 1644 there were estimated to be 255,000 Christians in China. Schall and his colleagues were imprisoned during a new persecution, and Schall died in prison, but the Emperor Kang Hsi studied mathematics with Schall's successor, Verbiest, and put an end to the persecution. In 1690 a Chinese Dominican, baptized as Gregory Lopez, became bishop of Nanking. He was the first Chinese bishop, and the only one until the twentieth century. But his consecration was a sign of a greater willingness to appoint national clergy than was shown by the Church either in the Philippines or the Americas. By 1695 there were seventy-five priests in China, half of them Jesuits.

Meanwhile, the missionaries in China became involved in a fierce disagreement over missionary methods, which lasted almost a hundred years. This dispute, known as the Chinese Rites Controversy, broke out when Franciscans and Dominicans protested against the concessions which Ricci and his colleagues had made to Chinese customs. The arguments in this dispute were very complicated, but in general Rome accepted the complaints, while the Chinese emperors sided with the Jesuits, and felt insulted at the questioning of Chinese ways, At one period the Emperor required all missionaries to follow the Jesuit practices. In the end the Church authorities condemned Ricci's ideas and activities completely. The reform of missionary methods pioneered by the Jesuits of China and India was then postponed until the twentieth century.

Toward the end of the eighteenth century the Christian population in China, which had reached about 250,000, ceased to increase. This slow-down resulted partly from the dissolution of the Jesuit order, and the confusion caused by the Rites Controversy, and partly from the decline of European support for missions during the French Revolution and its aftermath. A more important reason, however, was the stiffening resistance and hostility of the Chinese themselves, which led to some persecution. A great authority on missions to China, Professor K. S. Latourette, has commented:

To the orthodox Confucian scholars who made up the governing class, Christianity was subversive of much that was highest in Chinese civilization. . . . The wonder is, not that Christianity was persecuted, but that it was allowed to exist at all.

(*A History of Christian Missions to China*)

The Catholic Church in China did continue, however, and provided the base for a great expansion in the two centuries following.

KOREA AND JAPAN

The story of the beginnings of Christianity in *Korea* is very romantic and mysterious. The Jesuits in Peking became interested in that land, which paid tribute to the Chinese Emperor. A book by Ricci circulated there, and Schall secured permission from a Korean ruler to send missionaries there, but none was available to go at that time. The real beginning of the Church in Korea came in 1784, when a member of the Korean embassy in Peking was baptized. He returned to Korea, and taught others the Catholic faith. The Korean rulers were unfavourable, however, and some of the new Christians died for their faith in the following year.

But the Korean Christians persisted and secretly organized a Church, with bishops and priests. They baptized, confirmed, and said mass. Later some of them doubted their right to do these things, and asked for a priest to be sent from Peking. In 1794 a Chinese priest succeeded in entering Korea, and he worked there until he was discovered and executed in 1801. By that time the secret and persecuted Roman Catholic Church in Korea claimed some 10,000 members.

Japan during these centuries was the scene of an amazing success story of Christian evangelism. At the time of Francis Xavier's arrival, Japan was ripe for new things. The old feudal order was breaking down (see p. 85 and Vol. 2, p. 74), and the Japanese were interested in new ideas and new methods. Jesuit work on the Southern island of Kyushu was an immediate success. It has been estimated that thirty years after Francis Xavier's arrival there were 30,000 Japanese Christians, and ten years later the number had increased to 150,000. The first bishop arrived in 1596. By that time there were already two seminaries and 21 Japanese priests. The commander of the navy and the personal physician of the Shogun, or prime minister, were Christians.

But at the same time, the first wave of persecution broke out. The sad thing was that this persecution was partly caused by stories spread by Dutch merchants, who declared that the missionaries were agents of Spanish imperialism. The Dutch traders wanted no competition from Spaniards.

In 1601, the high point in early Catholic missionary work in Japan was reached; for example, nearly the entire population of the port city of Nagasaki had become Christian. But this success did not continue. Fierce and lasting persecution began in 1612, and was carried on with Japanese seriousness and thoroughness. Missionaries were expelled, and trade with Catholic countries—later with almost all countries— was stopped. There was strict censorship of books, and the death penalty was imposed for Church members. Christians were beheaded, crucified, and burned to death if they would not deny their faith. Any who did leave the Church were required to display certificates of membership in a Buddhist organization. As a result of this persecution, Buddhism became in effect the established religion of Japan. A party of Jesuits did manage to land secretly in 1642, but were discovered, tortured, and executed. For more than a century the entire population of Nagasaki was required to trample on the cross once a year. But amazingly enough, Christianity was not wiped out there, and the faith survived.

THE NEAR EAST

The Churches of the Near East were under Muslim rule during the entire period. The Turkish Empire was still expanding into Europe at this time, and the islands of Cyprus and Rhodes, which had earlier been ruled by orders of crusading knights, were conquered by the Turks. There were some cases of persecution of Christians by Muslims, but on the whole, Islam remained faithful to its principle of toleration for both Christians and Jews. However, the difficulties of being 'second class citizens' in a Muslim world were too much for many Christians, and there was a steady movement from the Church to Islam. Among the prominent Christians who became Muslims were members of the Byzantine royal family, the King of Georgia in what is now Russia, and the Metropolitan (Archbishop) of Rhodes.

One important way in which Christian groups maintained their identity in the face of Muslim predominance, was by submission to the Pope and the formation of Uniat Churches, such as the Maronite Church described in chapter 1 (p. 14). There were Roman Catholic Patriarchs of Antioch and Alexandria, and Uniat Coptic, Armenian, Jacobite, and Nestorian Churches. In each case some of the members remained true to their Orthodox allegiance, so the ecclesiastical map of the Near East became a very complicated one, and remains so today. It is said that today there are six different Patriarchs of Antioch belonging to these different Churches. The Uniat Churches with the largest number of members today are the Ruthenians and Ukrainians in south eastern Russia.

THE RUSSIAN ORTHODOX CHURCH

As Orthodoxy was suffering a decline in its ancient homelands in the Near East, the centre of Orthodox life and activity gradually shifted to Russia, and people began to speak of Moscow as the 'third Rome'. According to Orthodox belief, Rome itself had betrayed the faith through the new Roman Catholic teachings, which contradicted the ruling of ancient councils, and Constantinople, the 'New Rome', was in Muslim hands. Moscow indeed came to be recognized as one of the five Patriarchates of the Orthodox Church. The Church of Russia was a huge Church, but it is never very easy for the Church to grow in a poor land with a largely illiterate membership.

In the seventeenth century an attempt was made to purify the worship of the Church. For Orthodox Christians the liturgy is the central reality of the Christian life, and heaven and earth are brought together in every celebration of the liturgy. The continuous celebration of the true ('orthodox') liturgy of the ancient Church is held to be of the greatest importance.

A Patriarch of Moscow, whose name was Nikhon, had the Russian service books studied and compared with those of the Greek-speaking Church. He found that many errors had crept into the Russian service books as a result of copying, while important reforms had been made in the Greek liturgy. In 1666 he ordered a new Russian liturgy to be prepared, which would conform to the Greek practice. All those who opposed it were to be punished. For an illiterate people, who regarded the 'right' (*ortho* in Greek, hence 'orthodox') celebration of the liturgy as vital to salvation, these changes came as a great shock. Many refused to recognize the revised liturgy, and came to be known as 'Old Believers'.

These rebels soon divided into several different groups. A few continued to use the service of nonconforming priests, but the larger groups were 'priestless'. This latter group believed that the true Church had disappeared from the earth as a result of apostasy, and that the sacraments were no longer means of God's grace. Some held apocalyptic ideas, and thought that the changes in the liturgy were a sign that the second coming of Christ was near. Some of these volunteered for martyrdom, some burned their villages and committed suicide, some rebelled against the government, and others became Protestant. Some of these groups emigrated to North America.

Before very long another big change took place in the Russian Church. When Tsar Peter I, called 'the Great', came to the throne in 1699, he was determined to modernize Russian life and centralize the Russian government. He travelled in Western Europe to find out how things were being done there. Tsar Peter made French the language of the Russian court, and forced his nobles to shave off their beards. The pattern of 'modernization' practised in Europe at the end of the seventeenth century was absolute monarchy. And for a country to be really unified meant that it could not tolerate the existence of an institution which was wholly independent of the government, as the Church claimed to be, deriving its authority from God himself, independently of the Tsar. When the Patriarch of Moscow died in 1700, Peter the Great abolished his office. The Patriarchate was replaced by a 'Holy Synod', headed by a lawyer in government employment. In fact the Church became a government department.

It was under the Communist government in 1917 that the Patriarchate was restored to the Russian Church. The Orthodox Church in Communist Eastern Europe today has had much practice in living under very oppressive governments. Most Orthodox Churches lived under Muslim rule for centuries, and Muslim rule was followed by authoritarian Christian rulers who gave the Church little freedom of action.

Everywhere and always the Christian Church has been a missionary Church. When we remember its circumstances we can see that this is as true of the Eastern branch of the Church as of any other. Orthodox missionaries carried the Gospel to the Balkans and Russia. The Nestorians were for a time the predominant religious group in Central Asia, and carried the faith to China (see Vol. 2, chapter 4). From the middle of the seventeenth century the Muslim authorities forbade Orthodox Christians in the Near East and North Africa to preach their faith to others. But during the period we are studying, Russian Orthodox missionaries were hard at work. This was a time when Protestants were doing almost no missionary work beyond their own national boundaries.

As imperial Russia began to expand eastwards into Siberia, and across the Bering Straits into Alaska in North America, the Church moved as well. The Russian population of *Siberia*, which in 1600 had been about 70,000, had expanded to about a million by the end of the eighteenth century. By 1620 Tobolsk was an archbishopric with jurisdiction over the whole of Siberia, and Archbishop Leszczyski encouraged energetic mission work among the peoples of the region. A bishopric was established at Irkutsk and a seminary opened, which gave instruction in both the Chinese and Mongol languages. In 1750 it was announced that a majority of the local population of the Northern Siberian territory of Kamchatka had become Christian. The government strongly encouraged conversion, and excused converts from paying taxes for a set period of time.

Until 1863 Russian interests in Alaska were controlled by the Russian American Company. Its first two directors, Shelekov and Baranov, actively encouraged evangelism, and most of the Aleut Amerindians were baptized by the Orthodox Church. At first they adopted the religion of their conquerors, because they thought that a God who could save such cruel men as their Russian conquerors from eternal punishment must be remarkably powerful. Later, however, Father Innokenti Veniaminov, who worked for seven years among the Aleuts, learned their language, and laid the foundations of their anthropology, showed them something of the justice and mercy of the Father of Jesus Christ. The growth of the Church in both Siberia and Alaska, however, suffered from a lack of supervision and pastoral care.

From this brief survey we can see that the experience of the Church varied in different regions. But by 1800 a basis had been laid throughout Asia for the great evangelistic advances of the following century.

STUDY SUGGESTIONS

REVIEW OF CONTENT

1. By what method did de Nobili try to reach Hindus?
2. What was the Diamper Synod of the Syrian Orthodox Church?
3. What was the distinctive character of the Paris Mission?
4. What were the 'spiritual functions' of the Dutch United East India Company?
5. What is meant by the statement that the Church of the Indies was a 'company Church'?
6. What were the effects of the lack of pastors in Indonesia?
7. Why did so few Filipinos become priests before 1800?
8. What were Ricci's missionary methods?
9. What was the Rites Controversy, and what effects did it have on the Church in China?
10. Why did the Chinese so strongly resist Christian teaching?
11. How was the Christian faith brought to Korea?
12. Why did the Japanese government forbid the Christian religion?
13. Why did the Old Believers revolt against the Russian Orthodox Church?
14. In what ways did Peter the Great modernize the Russian Church?
15. Why did the Aleuts submit to baptism by the Russian Church?

DISCUSSION AND RESEARCH

16. The Christian Church has lived and grown under many different cultures and political systems, with more or less freedom. What is the minimum of freedom and protection necessary for the life of the Church? Must it have the recognition and protection of the government? Must it have the freedom to evangelize and influence the life of society directly?
17. The Church worships, preaches, teaches, witnesses, and evangelizes.

Rank these activities in order of importance. Are any missing? If your Church was failing or erring in any of them, would you feel justified in leaving the Church? Give examples to support your answer.

18. How far has 'modernization' affected the *ideas* of Church people in your country? How far has it changed the *activities* of the Church? Do you think these changes have been for good, or for bad? If the latter, what if anything can be done to improve the situation?

19. Have Christians in your country ever been persecuted: (a) by the government? (b) by other religious groups? If you yourself have ever been persecuted for your faith, what effect did it have on your faith?

CONCLUSION
The Foundations of the Worldwide Church

In the three hundred years which followed the year 1500, the foundations of modern society were laid. In the two centuries which followed
that, the ways of living and thinking which grew up during the period
covered in this volume were spread throughout the world. These
foundations were rooted in the three movements with which we began
our study (see p. 1). These were: (1) the New Learning, (2) European
sea-travel, and (3) the reform of the Church.

1. Most of the humanists who practised and spread the New Learning
remained Catholics, but they were dissatisfied with the way in which
the Roman Catholic Church responded to the Protestant Reformation.
These homeless intellectuals set the direction for modern science,
scholarship, technology, and philosophy, and the direction they took
was independent of official Christian theological thinking, either
Catholic or Protestant. A split developed between faith and reason,
religion and everyday life, and between the thinker and the world he
thought about. This split continues to puzzle Western thinkers today.
The more scholarship and science developed, the more people came to
agree with the seventeenth century French thinker, Michel de
Montaigne, who said: 'knowing much gives occasion for doubting more'.

2. The sea-voyages for trade which the Portuguese began in the
fourteenth century led gradually to the domination of the whole world
by Western Europeans. This process continued through the nineteenth
century, when Africa was divided up. The Dutch completed their
conquest of Indonesia, the French occupied Indo-China, and the English
took control of Burma. The agricultural revolution in Europe led to the
Industrial Revolution, in which the factories poured out more goods
than either the Europeans, or later the Americans, could use. Asia, Africa,
and Latin America became more important as markets for manufactured
goods from the West than as sources of gold, silver, spices, and silk.
As modern agriculture developed, Africa became the source of another
raw material; slaves for the vast plantations, especially in North America.

The Western dominance spread commerce, technology, and the slave
trade. It also provided new opportunities for spreading the Gospel.
Led by the Portuguese and Spanish, the Churches of the West, particularly the Roman Catholic Churches, preached, baptized and built
churches all over Latin America, in much of Asia, and parts of Africa.
The Philippines became a Christian archipelago. The Orthodox Church
of Russia spread the Gospel through Asian Siberia to Alaska.

German Pietists were the first pioneers of Protestant foreign missions, laying small beginnings in India. The great era of Protestant missions did not come until after 1800, but Protestantism was already spreading, not so much through evangelism, but as a result of the colonization of North America by English Christians, and the commercial settlements of the Protestant Dutch in East Asia. And the last five years of the eighteenth century saw the first beginnings of work by the London Missionary Society among the Pacific Island groups of Tahiti and Tonga.

3. The cleansing of the Church also divided it, and divided it again and again within Protestantism. The great theologians of the sixteenth century agreed among themselves on many of the most important questions, but they never produced a common creed. National Churches were the product of the Reformation, and the controversies within nations showed that it was possible—though not easy—for citizens of one nation to have different creeds. From two Churches in Luther's Germany, Protestantism went on to divide into dozens and later hundreds of denominations in the United States. Already in the seventeenth and eighteenth centuries a few Christians began to look for grounds on which the Churches could reunite.

Roman Catholics were as deeply concerned about the cleansing of the Church as the Protestants who separated from the Roman Church. The threat of division speeded up the process of reform, but it also made the Church defensive, more concerned about protecting its traditions than about responding creatively to the problems and challenges of the modern age. At the same time, of course, it was Catholics, not Protestants, who saw the expansion of the West into three other continents as an opportunity for evangelism, and who took full advantage of that opportunity.

And so a divided Church had inspired, but was also threatened by, the expansion of knowledge and the expansion of European influence. Now it faced the modern age, ushered in by colonialism, the Industrial Revolution, and modern scientific thinking. We may say that this modern period of human history began at the end of the eighteenth century, and that it started in France, where the feudal system was finally overcome by the French Revolution. The greatest relic of feudalism was eliminated when Napoleon dissolved the Holy Roman Empire in 1806.

The next advances of the Church were chiefly made by Protestants in North America and in mission fields around the world. The struggle of Christians with secular science and philosophy became intense and produced a new theology. In the future lay a worldwide Church, and new movements in evangelism, social work, worship, and theology to 'show forth the Lord's death until he come'.

'Protestant' Churches in Continental Europe	The Church in Great Britain	The Roman Catholic Church	'Missions' to Asia, Africa, and the Americas
		1502 Muslims expelled from Spain	1494 Demarcation of padroado
		1506 Rebuilding of St.Peter's Rome	1511 Portuguese seize Malacca
1516 Erasmus's Greek New Testament	1516 More's Utopia		1518 First priest in Ceylon
1517 Luther's 'Theses'		1519 Charles V Holy Roman Emperor	1519 Cortez conquers Mexico
1520 Luther's 'Open Letter'			1520 Henrique, first black African bishop
1521 Diet of Worms	1521 Henry VIII writes against Luther	1521 Hadrian VI, last non-Italian Pope	1521 Magellan in the Philippines
1521 Zwingli against the Mass			1524 French first in Canada
1524-26 Peasants' Revolt			1524 Priests to Mexico
1525 Anabaptism in Zürich	1526 Tyndale's English New Testament		
1525 Müntzer beheaded			
1527 Schleitheim Confession	1528 Patrick Hamilton, Scottish Protestant martyr	1527 Charles V sacks Rome	
1529 Diet of Speyer & Protestatio		1529 Ottoman Turks beseige Vienna	
1529 Marburg Colloquy	1530 Death of Wolsey		
1530 Augsburg Confession	1533 Henry VIII marries Anne Boleyn		
1530 Wars of Religion begin	1534 Henry VIII's Act of Supremacy		
1531 Zwingli killed in action	1534 Thomas More beheaded	1534 Pope Paul III	1534 France appointed 'protector' of Holy Places in Palestine
1534 Anti-catholic riots in France : Calvin imprisoned : Münster beseiged	1536 Dissolution of monasteries begins		
1536 Calvin's 'Institutes'			

'Protestant' Churches in Continental Europe

- 1536 Menno Simons joined Anabaptists
- 1539 Calvin expelled from Geneva
- 1545 Council of Trent opens
- 1546 Death of Luther
- 1549 Swiss Consensus on the Lord's Supper
- 1555 Peace of Augsburg
- 1559 First Synod of French Reformed Church
- 1562 Religious Wars in France begin
- 1572 Massacre of St Bartholomew in France
- 1577 Lutheran Formula of Concord
- 1594 End of Religious wars in France
- 1598 Edict of Nantes

The Church in Great Britain

- 1539 Parliament approves Six Articles
- 1539 All English monasteries confiscated
- 1547 Edward VI succeeds Henry VIII
- 1549 Cranmer's first Book of Common Prayer
- 1552 Cranmer's second BCP
- 1553 Mary Tudor - Catholic Queen
- 1556 Cranmer burned
- 1559 Elizabeth I's Act of Supremacy and Uniformity
- 1560 Church of Scotland established
- 1563-71 Thirty-nine Articles
- 1588 Spanish Armada defeated
- 1594 Hooker's Laws of Ecclesiastical Polity

The Roman Catholic Church

- 1540 Loyola's Society of Jesus recognized
- 1542 Pope Paul III sets up 'Holy Office' in Rome
- 1545 Copernicus' De revolutionibus
- 1545 Council of Trent opens
- 1552 Council of Trent, second session
- 1554 Charles V retires
- 1559 First Index
- 1563 Council of Trent adjourns
- 1582 Death of St Teresa of Avila

'Missions' to Asia, Africa, and the Americas

- 1537 Slavery prohibited in Mexico
- 1542 De las Casas' 'Laws of the Indies'
- 1542 Francis Xavier in Goa
- 1545 Francis Xavier in Japan
- 1548 Mexico an archdiocese
- 1552 Xavier again in Goa
- 1562 Slave trade begins
- 1565 Augustinians in the Philippines
- 1577 Franciscans in the Philippines
- 1582 Ruggieri and Ricci to China
- 1591 Manila an archdiocese
- 1599 Diamper Synod

'Protestant' Churches in Continental Europe		The Church in Great Britain		The Roman Catholic Church		'Missions' to Asia, Africa, and the Americas	
		1611	'Authorized' (King James) English Bible			1600	British East India Company chartered
						1602	Dutch East India Company founded
		1616	Congregational beginnings			1605	First Asian Protestant congregation at Ambon (Moluccas)
1618	Synod of Dort Netherlands					1606	Virginia company formed
1620	Hussites banned					1614	Persecution of Christians in Japan
		1624	Lord Herbert of Cherbury outlines 'Natural Religion'	1622	Roman 'Propaganda' founded	1620	Plymouth colony founded Massachusetts
				1625	St Vincent de Paul founds Lazarists		
1631	Swedes defeat Catholic Emperor in Germany			1633	St Vincent de Paul founds Sisters of Charity	1630	Massachusetts Bay colony founded
		1638	National Covenant in Scotland	1637	Descartes' Discourse on Method	1636	Harvard college opened
				1640	Cornelius Jansen's Augustinus	1637	Massachusetts expels Anne Hutchison
		1642-49	Civil War			1641	Dutch and English succeed Portuguese in Malacca
		1643	Westminster Confession				
		1645	Archbishop Laud executed			1644	Roger Williams receives Charter
1648	Peace of Westphalia	1649	Charles I executed			1646-48	Massachusetts adopts Westminster Confession
		1649-53	The Commonwealth				
		1650	George Fox founds Quakers				
				1657	Pascal's 'Provincial Letters'		
		1662	'King James' Book of Common Prayer	1671	Pascal's Pensées		

'Protestant' Churches in Continental Europe		The Church in Great Britain		The Roman Catholic Church		'Missions' to Asia, Africa, and the Americas	
1675	Spener's Pia Desideria						
1691	University of Halle founded						
		1695	Locke's 'Reasonableness of Christianity'	1685	Edict of Nantes revoked	1690	First Chinese bishop
		1688/9	Society for Promoting Christian Knowledge first British Missionary Society	1690	Gallican Articles condemned		
		1701	Society for the Propagation of the Gospel founded	1713	Jansenism condemned	1706	Pietist mission to Tranquebar
1727	Zinzendorf reorganizes Moravians as 'Brethren'						
1737	Zinzendorf bishop of Moravians	1739	John Wesley begins 'revival' preaching			1737	Revival in Northampton Massachusetts
						1740-44	The 'Great Awakening' in N.America
				1751	French Encyclopaedia Vols I and II	1744	Indian Christians condemn caste
						1768	Jesuits leave America
				1773	Jesuit Order suppressed		
1781	Kant's 'Critique of Pure Reason'					1785	Christian beginnings in Korea
				1789	The French Revolution	1791	American slaves returned to Freetown, Sierra Leone
		1794	Paley's 'Evidences'			1793	William Carey in India
		1795	Methodism a 'denomination'				
		1795	Tom Paine's 'Age of Reason'			1796	LMS missionaries in Tonga & Tahiti
		1795	LMS founded	1798	Napoleon imprisons the Pope		
		1799	CMS founded			1799	LMS work starts in South Africa

Key to Study Suggestions

CHAPTER 1

1. See p. 12, para. 2.
2. See p. 14, paras 3 and 4.
3. See p. 6, para. 5; p. 7, para. 2.
4. See p. 13, paras 2 and 3.
5. See especially pp. 3, 15, and 16.
6. See p. 12, para. 2.
7. See p. 2, para. 1; p. 3, para. 1; p. 4, paras 2 and 3.
8. See p. 4, para. 5.
9. See p. 6, numbered paras 1 and 2 and penultimate para.
10. See p. 6, last para. and p. 7, para. 1.
11. See p. 7, lines 19–10 from foot of page.
12. See p. 9, para. 2 including numbered items 1–3.
13. See p. 9, last 2 paras.
14. See p. 10, lines 14–23.
15. See p. 15, para. 2, lines 1–3.
16. See p. 11, paras 4 and 5.
17. See p. 17, lines 3–7.
18. See p. 13, last para. and p. 14, paras 1 and 2.
19. See p. 14, last para.

CHAPTER 2

1. See p. 19, para. 2.
2. See p. 25, last 9 lines and p. 26, lines 1 and 2.
3. See p. 18, para. 2.
4. See p. 18, last para.
5. See p. 19, last para. and p. 21, lines 1 and 2.
6. See p. 19, para 2.
7. See p. 21, last para.; p. 23, paras 1–3; p. 24, para. 2.
8. See p. 24, last 14 lines, and p. 25, lines 1 and 2.
9. See p. 26, lines 3–13, and last 6 lines.
10. (a) See p. 26, lines 14–24.
    (b) See p. 26, lines 25–34, and p. 28, lines 1–4.
11. See p. 28, lines 18–35.
12. See p. 28, last 6 lines, and p. 29, lines 1–4.

CHAPTER 3

1. See p. 39, lines 7–9.
2. See p. 40, numbered section 3, and explanatory para. following.
3. See p. 43, para. 1.
4. See p. 43, para. 4.
5. See p. 33, last para. and p. 34, lines 1–38.
6. See p. 35, paras 1 and 2.
7. See p. 36, para. 1.
8. See p. 36, para. 3.
9. (a) See p. 38, lines 18–21.
   (b) See p. 38, 1st para.
10. See p. 39, para. 3, last 5 lines.
11. See extract from the Schleitheim Confession, pp. 40, 42.
12. See p. 40, numbered section 4 and explanatory para. following.
13. See p. 40, lines 6–23.
14. See p. 43, paras 1–3.
15. See p. 44, para. 2.
16. See pp. 44 and 45, section headed 'The Radical Reformers' Continuing Influence'.
17. See p. 46, para. 2.
18. See p. 46, paras 5 and 6.
19. See p. 47, paras 1–3.

CHAPTER 4

1. See p. 52, para. 4, lines 1 and 2.
2. See p. 52, para. 4, lines 10–12.
3. See p. 53, para. 2, lines 5–10.
4. See p. 58, last para. and p. 65, para. 2.
5. See p. 62, numbered para. 2.
6. See p. 50, para. 1; p. 52, para. 2; p. 60, para. 2.
7. See p. 52, para. 4.
8. See p. 55, para. 3.
9. See p. 56, paras 2 and 3.
10. See p. 59, para. 3.
11. See p. 59, last 11 lines and p. 60, lines 1–21.
12. See p. 60, first para. after sub-heading, 'The Puritan Movement'.
13. See p. 61, penultimate para.
14. See p. 62, numbered paras 1–4.
15. See p. 65, line 15.
16. See p. 65, last para., lines 1 and 2.
17. See p. 64, numbered paras 1–4.

CHAPTER 5

1. See p. 67, paras 1 and 2.
2. See p. 68, paras 1 and 2.
3. See p. 73, para. 2.
4. See p. 75, line 10.
5. See p. 67, last 9 lines, and p. 76, para. 2.
6. See p. 70, para. 2.
7. See p. 70, penultimate para.
8. See p. 71, last para., and p. 73 first para.
9. See p. 73, last 3 paras, and p. 74, para. 1.
10. See p. 75, para. 1 (and also pp. 11 and 12).
11. See p. 75, section headed 'The Sacraments'.
12. See p. 71, para. 3; p. 75, last para.; and p. 76, para. 1.
13. See p. 74, Section headed 'The Bible'.

CHAPTER 6

1. See p. 81, lines 24, 25.
2. See p. 82, para. 3.
3. See p. 86, lines 8–12.
4. See p. 80, paras 1 and 2.
5. See p. 82, para. 1.
6. See p. 81, paras 1–3.
7. See p. 82, para. 4.
8. See p. 84, penultimate para, and p. 85, lines 1–11.
9. See p. 84, lines 13–15.
10. See p. 86, para. 2.
11. See p. 88, lines 9–15.
12. See p. 88, lines 14–12 from foot.
13. See p. 89, para. 3.
14. See p. 89, para. 4.
15. See p. 90, para. 3.
16. See p. 90, paras 4 and 5.

CHAPTER 7

1. See p. 97, lines 1 and 2.
2. See p. 96, para. 3.
3. See p. 100, lines 3–11.
4. See p. 93, paras 1 and 2.
5. See p. 93, para. 4, lines 1–4, and last para.
6. See p. 95, para. 2.

7. See p. 95, last para.

8. See p. 96, para. 4.

9. See p. 97, para. 1.

10. See p. 97, para. 2.

11. See p. 98, para. 4, lines 5–13.

12. See p. 100, last 3 lines, and p. 101, lines 1–6.

13. See p. 101, para. 3, lines 1–8.

14. See pp. 102, 103, section headed 'The Wall of Separation'.

CHAPTER 8

1. See p. 105, para. 3.

2. See p. 107, numbered para. 1.

3. See p. 107, numbered para. 2.

4. See p. 108, lines 23–28.

5. See p. 115, penultimate para.

6. See p. 105, last 2 paras, and p. 107, para. 1.

7. See p. 107, numbered paras 1 and 2.

8. See p. 107, numbered para. 1.

9. See p. 108, para. 1 (numbered 2).

10. See p. 108, para. 2 (numbered 3).

11. See p. 108, para. 2 (numbered 3).

12. See p. 109, penultimate para., and p. 110, para. 2.

13. See p. 110, paras 1 and 3.

14. See p. 111, section headed 'University of Halle'.

15. See p. 111, last two paras, and p. 112, paras 1–3.

16. See p. 115, lines 3–22.

17. See p. 115, lines 23–35, and last 2 lines; and p. 116, lines 1–9.

CHAPTER 9

1. See p. 123, lines 2–6.

2. See p. 123, para. 4, lines 1–5.

3. See p. 122, last 3 lines, and p. 123, lines 1, 2, and last 4 lines.

4. See p. 118, paras 1 and 2.

5. See p. 118, para. 3, lines 3–5.

6. See p. 120, para. 2.

7. See p. 120, last 4 lines, and p. 121, lines 1–7.

8. See p. 121, last 2 paras, and p. 122, lines 1–4, and para. 4.

9. See p. 124, paras 1–3.

10. See p. 124, last 2 paras.

CHAPTER 10

1. See p. 128, lines 2–22.
2. See p. 129, lines 6–9.
3. See p. 130, lines 2–5.
4. See p. 130, lines 18–25.
5. See p. 130, last para, and p. 131, lines 1–3.
6. See p. 131, paras 3 and 4.
7. See p. 131, last para., and p. 132, lines 1–26.
8. See p. 133, paras 2 and 4.
9. See p. 135, para. 3.
10. See p. 133, para. 3, and p. 136, lines 1–4.
11. See p. 136, para. 2.
12. See p. 136, last para.
13. See p. 138, para. 3.
14. See p. 138, last para, and p. 139, para 1.
15. See p. 139, last 3 lines, and p. 140, para. 1.

Index

Act of Supremacy, 52, 59
Act of Uniformity, 64
Adams, John, 102
Affonzo, 14
Africa, 14, 142
Age of Reason, Paine's, 108
Akhbar, 127
Alaska, 139, 140, 142
Aleuts, 139, 140
Alexander VI, Pope, 14, 81
Alexandria, 1
Alphonsus Liguori, 120, 121
America, Latin, 14, 142
America, North 1, 39, 82, 85, 89, 90
America, South, 1, 39, 82, 85
Amerindians, 86, 88, 90, 112, 124, 139
Anabaptists, 15, 34, 39–43, 47, 100
Anglicans, 62, 100, 115
Angola, 80
Antinomianism, 96
Antioch, 1, 137
Apocrypha, 74
Apostolic succession, 24
Armada, the, 58
Armenian Churches, 137
Articles, Forty-two, 59
Articles, Six, 55
Articles, Thirty-nine, 59, 97
Asia, 127, 142, 143
Augsburg (Augustana), Confession, 12; Diet of, 12; Peace of, 31, 39
Augustinians, 88
Augustinus, Jansen's, 121
Austria, 18, 31, 124
'Awakening', *see* 'Great Awakening'
Aztecs, 82, 84, 86

Babylonian Captivity of the Church, The, Luther's, 9
Balkans, 14
Baptism, doctrine of, 38–40
Baptists, 62, 100, 101

Baranov, 139
Baroque art, 75
Basle, 21
Batavia, 130
Bellarmino, Cardinal, 24, 127
Bengal, 128
Bernard of Clairvaux, 13
Bethlehem, Pennsylvania, 112
Bible, 'Authorized' or 'King James' version, 61
Biblical teaching, 3, 9, 13, 18, 19, 74
Biblical theologians, 23
Bloody Tenet, Cotton's, 102
Boleyn, Anne, 52, 55
Bondage of the Will, On the, Luther's, 11
Book of Common Prayer, 55, 56, 64, 65
Book of Martyrs, Foxe's, 58
Bora, Katherine von, 11
Brazil, 81, 88
Brethren, The, 111, 112
British East India Company, 50
Browne, Robert; Browneites, 62
Bucer, Martin, 25, 46, 60
Bunyan, John, 100
Burma, 130, 142

Calvin, John, 11, 21, 23–29, 40, 44, 47, 60
'Cambridge Platform', 97
Canada, 89
Carey, William, 128
Casas, Bartolomeo de las, 86
Catherine of Aragon, Queen, 52
Catholic Reformation, 67, 68, 122
Central America, 86
Ceremonies, 118
Ceylon, 84, 90, 124, 129, 130
Chalcedon, 1
Charles I of England, 61, 92
Charles V, Holy Roman Emperor, 16, 31, 52, 74
China, 1, 80, 85, 132, 133, 135
Chinese Rites controversy, 135

Christendom, 1, 3, 31
'Christian Church', 102
Christian Liberty, Treatise on, Luther's, 10
Church, doctrine of the, 24
Church government, 3, 25, 99, 123
Church of England, 62, 114
Church of the Indies, 130
Circuit Riders, 116
Civil War in England, 61, 62, 96
Claver, Peter, 88
Clement VII, Pope, 52
Clement XIV, Pope, 124
Colet, John, 53
Colombia, 88
Colonization, colonialism, 90, 92, 143
Columbus, Christopher, 82, 85
Common Prayer, Book of, 55, 56, 60, 64, 65
'Commonwealth', The, 61, 62
Communion Service, 56
Communism, 114, 139
Concord, Formula of, Lutheran, 109
Confessions, Augsburg (Augustana), 12, 109; Gallican, 109; Schleitheim, 40, 43; Scottish, 109; Westminster, 65, 97
Confucianism, 133, 136
Congo, 14
Congregationalists, 62
Congregation of the Index, 73
Congregational organization, 39, 40, 97
Conquistadors, 82
Constantinople, 1, 138
Copernicus, 76
Coptic Churches, 137
Cortez, Hernando, 82, 84, 85
Cotton, John, 102
Council of Trent, 73, 74, 77
Councils of the Church, rule by, 9, 15, 16, 31, 67, 123
Counter Reformation, 67
Coverdale, Miles, 52
Cranach, Lucas, 8
Cranmer, Thomas, 52, 55, 56, 58, 63, 64
Cromwell, Oliver, 61, 62
Cromwell, Thomas, 53, 55
Czechoslovakia, 33

Deism, Deists, 108
Denmark, 11, 31
Denominationalism, 98–100, 102
Deutsche Messe, Luther's, 46
Dialogue of Comfort, More's, 53
Diamper Synod, 129
Diaz, Bernal, 82
Diet of the Holy Roman Empire, 7, 10, 12
Discipline, 40
Dogmatics, 109
Dominicans, 85, 88, 124, 135
Dort, Synod of, 33
Dutch East India Company, 89, 90, 130

Eastern Churches, 14, 139
East Indies, 14, 130
Eck, John, 35
Ecumenical Council, 73
Ecumenical Movement, 2
Edward VI of England, 55, 56, 64
Edwards, Jonathan, 97, 98, 114
Elizabeth I of England, 58, 59
Elizabethan Settlement, 59
Empiricists, 107
Encyclopaedia, The, 108
Engels, 114
England, 33, 50; Church of, 62, 114
Ephesus, 1
Erasmus, Desiderius, 4–6, 11, 19
Ethiopia, 1
Eugene IV, Pope, 25
European outreach, 15
Eusebius, 34
'Evangelical Rationalists', 34, 43, 44
'Evangelicals', 12, 18, 21
Evidences of Christianity, Paley's, 107
Excommunication, 40
Exploration, 90

Faith, doctrine of, 7, 18
Feudalism, 15, 36
'First Amendment, the', 103
Formosa (Taiwan), 90
Formula Missae, Luther's, 46
Formula of Concord, Lutheran, 109
Fox, George, 101
Foxe, John, 55, 58

France, 31, 33, 89, 124
Francis of Assisi, 13
Francis Xavier, 76, 84, 85
Franciscans, 1, 85, 86, 88, 124, 129, 135
Franke, August Hermann, 111
Franklin, Benjamin, 100, 102, 103
Frederick III of Saxony, 10
'Free Church', 43, 44
French Revolution, 125, 135
Friends, Society of, 101

Galileo, 76
Gallican Articles (Liberties), 123
Gallican Confession, 109
Gallicanism, 122, 123
Gama, Vasco da, 80
General Councils (of the Church), 3, 67, 73
Geneva, 21–23, 28, 44, 47
Germany, 4, 15, 19, 25, 31, 33, 39, 105
Goa, 80, 84, 85, 127, 128
Government, of the Church, 3, 60
Grace, doctrine of, 12, 13
'Great Awakening', 98, 101, 113, 114
Great Schism, 67
Grebel, Conrad, 34, 39
Grey, Lady Jane, 56–58
Guaraní, 88, 124

Hadrian VI, Pope, 67
Halle, University of, 111
Hampton Court Conference, 61
Hapsburgs, 16, 74
Harvard College, 95
Hawkins, John, 50
Henrique, Bishop in Congo, 14
Henry IV of France, 33
Henry VIII of England, 11, 51–56, 62, 64
Herbert, Lord, of Cherbury, 108
Heresy, 73
'High Churchmen', 61
Hinduism, 127
Hoffmann, Melchior, 43
Holy Office, 71, 73
Holy Roman Empire, 9, 19, 25, 105, 143
'Holy Synod' (Russian), 139
Hooker, Richard, 59, 60
Hope, doctrine of, 45

Hsu, Paul, 135
Hübmaier, Balthazar, 34, 39
Huguenots, 33
Humanism, Humanists, 11, 21, 26, 105
Hungary, 14, 33
Huss, John, 4, 7, 10
Hutchison, Anne, 96

Ignatius of Antioch, 13, 68
Ignatius Loyola, 68–70, 76, 84
Incas, 82
'Independents', 62
Index, 67, 73
India, 1, 14, 80, 84, 127, 128
'Indo-China', 130, 142
Indonesia, 80, 90, 130, 131, 142
Industrial Revolution, 114, 142, 143
'Inner Mission', 111
Inquisition, 67, 71, 73
Institutes of the Christian Religion, Calvin's, 21, 23, 24
Invincible Armada, 58
Iranaeus of Lyons, 24
Irkutsk, 139
Islam, 1, 80, 127, 137
Italy, 31, 33, 121

Jacobite Churches, 129, 137
Jakarta, 131
James I of England, 61
James V of Scotland, 65
Jansen, Cornelius, 121, 122
Jansensism, Jansensists, 121, 122
Japan, 80, 84, 85, 136, 137
Java, 90
Jefferson, Thomas, 102
Jerusalem, 1
Jesuits, 68, 70, 71, 84–86, 121, 122, 124, 128, 132, 133, 135–137
John of the Cross, 75
Justification, doctrine of, 7, 12, 29, 74, 96

Kamchatka, 139
Karlstadt, Andreas, 26, 34, 35, 44
Knox, John, 65
Korea, 136

Languages, 3, 46
Latin America, 14, 82
Laud, Archbishop, 61
Laws of Ecclesiastical Polity, Hooker's, 59
Laws of the Indies, 86
Lazarist Order, 120
Lebanon, 14
Lefèvre d'Étaples, Jacques, 6, 21
Leipzig, 7; Leipzig Disputation, 35
Leo X, Pope, 9
Leszczyski, Archbishop, 139
'Levellers', 62
Liguori, Alphonsus, 120
Liturgy, changes in, 35, 46, 47, 76, 138
Loci Communes, Melanchthon's, 13
Locke, John, 107, 108
Lombard, Peter, 24
London Missionary Society, 143
Lopez, Gregory, 135
Lord's Supper, doctrine of, 9, 25, 26, 28, 29, 40, 46, 56–58, 75, 122
Louis XIV of France, 106, 123
Louvain, 121
'Low Church' party, 115
Loyola, Ignatius, 68–70, 76, 84
Luther, Martin, 3–13, 18, 24–26, 31, 34–36, 39, 46, 75, 76
Lutherans, 18, 39, 47, 100
'Lutheran Spiritualists', 34, 35, 38

Macao, 14, 80, 85, 132
Mactan Is, 88
Magellan, Ferdinand, 14, 82, 88
'Magisterial' Reformation, 33, 44
Malabar, 1, 14; Malabar Church, 128, 129
Malacca, 14, 80, 84, 85, 89, 129
Manz, Felix, 39
Marburg, 25
Maronite Church, 14
Marriage, Luther's teaching on, 12
Martyrs' Mirror, 39
Marx, Karl, 114
Mary Queen of Scots, 65
Mary Tudor, 56, 58
Massachusetts Bay Colony, 95, 96
Mathijs, Jan, 43

Melanchthon, Philip, 11, 12, 25
Mennonites, 43
Merit, doctrine of, 6
Methodists, 100, 115, 116
Mexico, 14, 85, 86
Middle Ages, 105
Mindanao, 131
Minister, office of, 40
'Missions', 120, 124, 125, 131, 137, 143
'Modernization', 139
Moghul Empire, 14, 127, 129, 132
Moluccas, 14, 80, 84, 85, 89, 130
Monasteries, 55
Money-economy, development of, 15
Monks, 68
Monophysites, 129
Montaigne, Michel de, 142
Montezuma, 84
Moral Reflections, Quesnal's, 122
Moravians, 112
More, Thomas, 52–54
'Moros', 131
Münster, 43; Münster, Peace of, *see* Westphalia
Müntzer, Thomas, 34–38, 45

Nagasaki, 137
Nantes, Edict of, 33
Nations, development of, 15
'Natural' Religion, 108, 118
Near East, 137
Neri, Philip, 76
Nestorians, 1, 129, 137, 139
Netherlands, 33, 39, 89
Netherlands United East India Company, 89, 90
New England, 97
'New Learning', 1–4, 11, 142
'New Men', 16
New Testament, 4
Nicene Creed, 24
Nikhon, Patriarch of Moscow, 138
Ninety-five Theses, Luther's, 7
Nobili, Roberto de, 127, 128, 133
North America, 1, 89, 92, 143
Norway, 31

Obedience, doctrine of, 42

Ockham, William of, 50
Old Catholic Church, 122
Open Letter, Luther's, 9
Orthodox Churches, 137–139, 142
Osiander, Andreas, 55
Osnabruck, *see* Westphalia
Ottoman Turks, 14

Pacific, 1, 143
Padroado, 81, 87, 124, 127
Paine, Thomas, 108
Paley, William, 107
Papacy, 71; *see also* Popes
Papal States, 71
Paraguay, 85, 88, 124
Paris Mission, 130
Pascal, Blaise, 122
Passionist Order, 120
'Patronage', 81, 87
Paul III, Pope, 71, 72, 73
Paul VI, Pope, 73
Paul of the Cross, 120
Paulus, Ly, 134
Peasant uprisings, 15, 38
Penance, 75
Penn, William, 101
Pennsylvania, 101
Pereira, Julian, 127
Peru, 14, 83
Peter the Great, Tsar, 138
Philip II of Spain, 58
Philip IV of France, 4
Philippines, 14, 81, 85, 88, 89, 131, 132, 142
Pia Desideria, Spener's, 110
Pietism, Pietists, 109–111, 143
Pizarro, Francisco, 82, 83
Plantagenets, 40
Plymouth Colony, 92–94
Poland, 33, 39
Pole, Cardinal Reginald, 58
'Poor Men of Lyons', 4
Popes, power of, 3, 9, 71, 73, 81, 82, 123
Port-Royal, 122
Portugal, Portuguese, 14, 15, 30–32, 82, 124, 129, 142
Prayer Book, Common, 55, 56, 64, 65
Predestination, doctrine of, 19

Presbyterians, 62, 65, 97, 100
Protestantism, Protestants, 2, 18, 75, 109, 142
Protestatio, 12
Provincial Letters, Pascal's, 122
Prussia, 124
Puritans, 60, 61, 92, 97, 99

Quakers, 62, 100, 101
Quesnal, Pasquier, 122

Radical humanists, 19
Radical Reformation, 11, 33–35, 44, 60, 62
'Rational Religion', 102, 107, 118
Rationalists, 107
Reasonableness of Christianity, Locke's, 108
'Re-baptism', 39
Redemptorist order, 120
Reform, 2, 142
Reformation, 2, 4, 6, 7, 11, 12, 15, 28, 36, 67, 71, 73, 75, 76, 142
Reformed, the, 18, 19, 23, 65, 100; Reformed Churches, 21, 28
Reformers, 24
'Regular Clerks', 68
Religion, wars of, 33, 105, 107
Religious Affections, Edwards', 98
Renaissance, 1
Restitutio Christianismi, Servetus's, 44
Reuchlin, Johannes, 6
Revival, 98, 114, 115
Rhode Island, 96
Rhodes, 137
Ricci, Matteo, 133–136
Roman Catholic Church, 2, 24, 26, 28, 67, 76, 100, 125, 142, 143
Roman Empire, 1
Ruggieri, Michael, 132, 133
Rumania, 33
Russia, 1, 39, 124, 137–139
Russian American Company, 139
Russian Orthodox Church, 138, 142

Sacraments, doctrine of, 9, 10, 75
Sacred Heart, devotions to, 118, 121
Sadoleto, Cardinal Jacopo, 28
Salazar, Domingo de, 88

Saxony, 36
Schall, Adam von Bell, 135, 136
Schleitheim Confession, 40, 43
Science, 105, 106, 142, 143
Scotland, 33, 50; Scotland, Church of, 65
Sea-voyages, 1, 142
Sentences, Peter Lombard's, 24
Separation (of Church and State), 103
Separation, practice of, 40, 42
Separatists, 62, 92
Serbia, 14
Servetus, Miguel, 34, 37, 43, 44
Seymour, Jane, 55
Shakespeare, William, 59
Shelekov, 139
Siberia, 139, 140, 142
Simons, Menno, 43
Simony, 73
Sisters of Charity, 120
Six Articles, 55
Slave trade, 50, 86, 142
Social change, 15
Society of Friends, 101
Society of Jesus, 68, 71, 84
Society for Promoting Christian Knowledge, 129
South America, 1, 82
South East Asia, 129
South India, 1, 128
Spain, Spanish, 1, 14, 15, 31, 80–82, 85, 124, 131, 142
Spener, Jacob, 109–111
Speyer, Diet of, 12
Spiritual Exercises, Loyola's, 70, 71
'Spiritualists', Lutheran, 34
Stations of the Cross, 120
St Bartholomew's Day Massacres, 31
Strasbourg, 46, 47
Suffering, doctrine of, 45
Sunday worship, 47
Supremacy, Act of, 52, 59
Swearing, 42
Sweden, 31
Switzerland, 11, 18, 19, 33
Sword, Doctrine of, 40
Syrian Orthodox Church, 14, 127–129

Tahiti, 143
Teresa of Avila, 75, 76
Thailand, 130
Theology, dogmatic, 109, 110
Theses, Luther's Ninety-five, 7
Thirty-nine Articles, 97
Thirty Years' War, 31, 105, 112
Tibet, 132
Timor, 14, 130
Tindal, Matthew, 108
Tobolsk, 139
Tonga, 143
Tranquebar, 129
Transubstantiation, doctrine of, 25, 26, 75
Trent, Council of, 73, 75–77
Troeltsch, Ernst, 99
Tudor, House of, 50
Turkestan, 132
Turks, 14, 77, 89, 137
Tyndale, William, 50

Ultramontanism, 123
Uniat Churches, 14, 129, 137
Uniformity, Act of, 64, 65
United East India Company, 89, 90, 130
United States, 143
Uruguay, 85, 88, 124
Utopia, More's, 53

Vasco da Gama, 80
Veniaminov, Innokenti, 140
Verbiest, 135
Vienna, 14
Vincent de Paul, 118–120
Virginia Colony, 92, 93
Voltaire, 124, 125
Vulgate, 74, 75

Waldensians, 33, 35
'Wall of Separation', 103
Wars of Religion, 33, 105, 107
Wartburg, 10, 34
Wesley, Charles, 112
Wesley, John, 100, 112–115
West Indies, 14, 85, 90
Westminister Confession, 65, 97
Westphalia, Peace of, 31, 39

Whitefield, George, 113, 114
Whitgift, John, 61
Williams, Roger, 95, 96, 102
Wittenberg, 3, 7, 10, 34, 35
Wolsey, Thomas, 52, 53
Worms, Diet of, 7
Wycliffe, John, 4, 10, 25, 35, 47

Xavier, Francis, 76, 84, 85, 136

Yale, 98

Zinzendorf, Nikolaus von, 111, 112
Zumarraga, 86
Zürich, 38, 39
Zwingli, Ulrich, 11, 19–21, 25, 28, 38–40, 46